COMMON CULTURE

COMMON CULTURE

Symbolic work at play in the everyday cultures of the young

PAUL WILLIS
with Simon Jones, Joyce Canaan
and Geoff Hurd

OPEN UNIVERSITY PRESS
Milton Keynes

Open University Press
Celtic Court
22 Ballmoor
Buckingham
MK18 1XW

First Published 1990

British Library Cataloguing in Publication Data
Willis, Paul
    Common culture: Symbolic work at play in the everyday cultures
    of the young.
    1. Young persons culture
    I. Title
    306

    ISBN 0-335-09432-5
    ISBN 0-335-09431-7 (pbk.)

Typeset by Rowland Phototypesetting Limited
Bury St Edmunds, Suffolk
Printed in Great Britain by
J. W. Arrowsmith Limited, Bristol

Contents

Chapters 3 and 4 were written by Simon Jones and edited by Paul Willis. Chapter 5 was written by Joyce Canaan, rewritten and edited by Paul Willis.

Preface and acknowledgements

The writing of this book has grown out of and draws from the findings of an enquiry into the cultural activities of young people initiated and generously financed by the Gulbenkian Foundation. This enquiry was conducted during 1987 and 1988, directed by myself, administered and academically advised by Geoff Hurd. The School of Humanities and Cultural Studies at Wolverhampton Polytechnic housed and sympathetically supported the project throughout. An end-of-grant report and a summary were published by the Gulbenkian Foundation.

The spine of the Gulbenkian enquiry was a twelve-month ethnographic and interview research project, conducted in Wolverhampton, mainly by Joyce Canaan, during which a large number of discussions were taped with different groups of young people. At the same time some fifteen separate studies were commissioned on a national basis covering a wide range of young people's cultural activities usually involving substantial further ethnographic work ranging in location from Sunderland to London.

I have drafted most of this book and have edited and directed its production. I take responsibility for the basic arguments yet the book is in many ways the result of a collective enterprise – even when some of those involved may disagree, sometimes profoundly, with what it finally says. Several of the commissions for the Gulbenkian enquiry have been drawn on generally and in specific ways. These are listed in the Appendix to this book. The TV and the magazine sections of chapter 2 draw more directly and continuously on the submissions by Graham Murdock and Janice Winship respectively. At my request Simon Jones wrote up chapters 3 and 4, drawing together his own and other work completed for the enquiry. Chapter 5 is a redraft by me of Joyce Canaan's original field report.

The book has also benefited directly from extensive discussions and consultations in regular meetings between myself, Geoff Hurd, Joyce Canaan and Simon Jones, and from textual commentary and criticism from a variety of other individuals including Phil Corrigan (to whom particular thanks for extended written comments), Kim Taylor (to whom particular thanks for initiating the original enquiry as then Director of the Gulbenkian Foundation, and for following through with such active support), Stephen Yeo, Huw Beynon, Michael Green, Celia Lury, Simon Richey and Doug Foley. Josie Wall has worked wonders in typing up reams of delphic script.

Thanks to all these, but most importantly, thanks to the young people whose words we use and whose creative activities we try to represent.

Paul Willis

Some recent statistics

5% of the UK population attend the theatre, opera or ballet.

4% of the UK population attend museums or art galleries.

2% of the UK working class attend any of the above.

2% of all young people (excluding students) attend the theatre (the most popular traditional arts venue).

0% of the young unemployed attend the theatre.

98% of the population watch TV on average for over 25 hours a week.

92% of 20–24-year-olds listen to the radio.

87% of 20–24-year-olds listen to records/tapes.

75% of 16–24-year-olds go to pubs on average about four times a week.

40% of 16–24-year-olds go to the cinema at least once in three months.

38% of 11–25-year-olds go to discos.

26% of 11–25-year-olds go to nightclubs.

Whilst cultural statistics are notoriously patchy and difficult to compare, the above is a fair reflection of what is available. Unless otherwise stated, statistics refer to visits or activities undertaken within a four week period. Sources: *General Household Survey* 1983 and 1986; *Cultural Trends* (PSI), 1989; *The Youth Review* (P. Willis *et al.*, Avebury), 1988; The *Smash Hits* Youth Survey, 1985.

— 1 —
Symbolic creativity

The institutions and practices, genres and terms of high art are currently categories of exclusion more than of inclusion. They have no real connection with most young people or their lives. They may encourage some artistic specializations but they certainly discourage much wider and more general symbolic creativity. The official existence of the 'arts' in institutions seems to exhaust everything else of its artistic contents. If some things count as 'art', the, rest must be 'non-art'. Because 'art' is in the 'art gallery', it can't therefore be anywhere else. It is that which is special and heightened, not ordinary and everyday.

The arts establishment, by and large, has done little to dispel these assumptions. It prefers instead to utilize or even promote fears of cultural decline and debasement in order to strengthen its own claims for subsidy, institutional protection and privilege. In general the arts establishment connives to keep alive the myth of the special, creative individual artist holding out against passive mass consumerism, so helping to maintain a self-interested view of élite creativity.

Against this we insist that there is a vibrant symbolic life and symbolic creativity in everyday life, everyday activity and expression – even if it is sometimes invisible, looked down on or spurned. We don't want to invent it or propose it. We want to recognize it – literally re-cognize it. Most young people's lives are not involved with the arts and yet are actually full of expressions, signs and symbols through which individuals and groups seek creatively to establish their presence, identity and meaning. Young people are all the time expressing or attempting to express something about their actual or potential *cultural significance*. This is the realm of living common culture. Vulgar sometimes, perhaps. But also 'common' in being everywhere, resistant, hardy. Also 'common' in being shared, having things 'in common'. Where 'arts' exclude, 'culture' includes. 'Art' has been cut short of meanings, where 'culture' has not.

As Raymond Williams always insisted, culture is ordinary.[1] It is the extraordinary in the ordinary, which is extraordinary, which makes both into culture, common culture. We are thinking of the extraordinary symbolic creativity of the multitude of ways in which young people use, humanize, decorate and invest with meanings their common and immediate life spaces and social practices – personal styles and choice of clothes; selective and active use of music, TV, magazines; decoration of bedrooms; the rituals of romance and subcultural styles; the style, banter and drama of friendship groups; music-making and dance. Nor are these pursuits and activities trivial or inconsequential. In conditions of late modernization and the widespread crisis of cultural values they can be crucial to the creation and sustenance of individual and group identities, even to cultural survival of identity itself. There is work, even desperate work, in their play.

The arts institution

The existence, reproduction and appreciation of the high arts or 'official arts' depends on institutions, from individual art galleries, museums, theatres, ballet companies to the Arts Council itself. But institutions include not only buildings and organizations, but also systematic and specific social values and practices. The appreciation of official art (its consumption) further depends on the acquisition of certain kinds of knowledge and therefore on a prior educational process lodged within its own kinds of institutions. That is, the taste for art is learned.

The conventional list of 'high art' includes classical music, ballet, opera, drama, poetry, literature, the visual and plastic arts. Within these branches of art are institutionalized canons which attempt to place the 'works' into finite hierarchies differentiating greater and lesser value. Of course these hierarchies are not fixed. In contradiction to the sense of the universal which is supposed to characterize 'great art', new works (by no means always newly created) are admitted over time, just as established ones slip down or out. But at all times there are a limited number only of 'great works'.

These different aspects of the institutionalization of art produce the physical organizational and cultural separation of 'art', but also the possibility of an *internal* 'hyperinstitutionalization' of 'art' – the complete dissociation of art from living contexts. This is where the merely formal features of art can become the guarantee of its 'aesthetic', rather than its relevance and relation to real-life processes and concerns: religious art installed in the antiseptic stillness of the museum. In the 'hyperinstitutionalization' of 'art', aesthetic appreciation can become so atrophied as to make culturedness only the knowledge of form. Expressions and artefacts become inert things. Seated in the opera stalls, knowing what to expect again, seeing themselves reflected all around, the élite may actually be bored through and through with only the shell of that which used to contain a passion of meaning.

When aesthetic communication and critique become rhetorical assemblies of clever allusions and of wholly self-contained and therefore usually vacuous artistic 'cross references', 'art' can end up in a floating and sometimes charlatan aesthetic without its own associated human practices and transformations. But this floating aesthetic conceals the social process by which it is appreciated, a process relying largely on the prior institutions of liberal-arts education to supply the knowledge of the purely formal and internal history of 'art'. And here lies the rub, for in the hyperinstitutionalization of 'art' the 'others', the 'uncultured', merely lack the code, but they're seen and may sometimes see themselves as ignorant, insensitive and without the finer sensibilities of those who really 'appreciate'. Absolutely certainly they're not the 'talented' or 'gifted', the élite minority held to be capable of performing or creating 'art'.

The traditional function of the artist is seen to be in the production of a refined aesthetic in things, texts and artefacts. Cultural practices involve, to be sure, symbolic representations, and part of their creativity is in the critical and creative transformation of these representations. But representational work cannot claim the distinction of being involved in a creative aesthetic unless it is in some real productive relationship to what is represented, unless it is embedded in a process of consciousness and meaning-making – categories which are not 'internally coded' but are a result of symbolic creativity. The notion of the full-time artist – separate from the market and requiring subsidy – is, if anything, at the periphery of the field of symbolic creativity in common culture, not at its centre. But it can seem to be its centre, thus disorienting the whole field with respect to its own real cultural practices and functions. Furthermore it may be that certain kinds of symbolic creativity in the expressive and communicative activity of 'disadvantaged' groups exercise their uses and economies in precisely eluding and evading formal recognition, publicity and the possible control by others of their own visceral meanings. In this case the decontextualized search for aesthetics is, by definition, doomed to endless labour, for the aesthetic will be wherever it isn't. Hyper-institutionalization excludes but can also repel.

It seemed for a time that things might be different. In the phase of social reconstruction after the war, part of the welfare–capitalist pact was to widen out the appreciation and practice of the high arts from their traditional base in the leisured upper-middle class. The arts were part of those good things of life which were to be shared out more equally. As in other areas, the state was to be responsible for this sharing out. The formation of the Arts Council in 1945 and the BBC Third Programme in 1946 was to spearhead this democratization of the arts. But the 'raise and spread' motto didn't last very long or spread very far. The Arts Council withdrew very promptly from the sites of popular consumption, cutting back promotions in Butlin's holiday camps, exhibitions in schools, canteens, factories and shops. Local arts clubs, regional initiatives, subsidized symphonies – many of these too were soon abandoned.

In fact the state became the vehicle for the continuance and reinforcement of the traditional conceptions and institutions of high culture rather than a vehicle for cultural democratization and experimentation with new, altogether wider institutions. The 'spreading' of art became highly specific and essentially conservative: the leisure-class idea of 'good culture' maintained its dominance (if not the class itself) but with now a wider well-subsidized audience of the rising middle class of managers and professionals.

The current attempts by the Conservative government to abrogate the 1945 welfare pact, specifically in the cultural field, by forcing the arts to reconstitute themselves in market terms does not really attack the continuing minority basis, élite and exclusive definition of the high arts. It merely seeks to lessen or to remove their state subsidies – or even bring back patronage in the form of high-class corporate-image enhancement. If the post-1945 welfare-state arts policy had really been about democratic cultural development, if it had not given up so early on imaginative alternatives, if it had not so easily taken over the leisure-class view of art, then the current opposition to the government's cultural pre-Keynesianism might, itself, be much more broadly based.

Though subordinated and often marginalized, the many strands of the community arts movement continue to carry the torch. They share the continuing concern to democratize the arts and make them more a part of common experience. Their search for new or expanded publics can, however, suffer from the implicit assumption that such groups are, in some sense, 'non-publics', that they have no forms of their own, no culture, no common culture, except perhaps a very much debased version of élite culture or of mass culture passively consumed. There can be a final unwillingness and limit even in subversive or alternative movements towards an arts democracy. They may have escaped the physical institutions and academies, but not always their conventions – the forms must be kept more or less intact. If they must go, then so too does any notion of a specifically artistic practice. What is left is indistinguishable from other activities such as community action or politics itself. Some activists are, indeed, led by this logic to pure community action. But an approach which won't discard the conventions makes assumptions which presuppose effects which must be free. If it is to be free, creative activity must be allowed to be what it is, and to lead where it will.

There seem to be hidden questions behind even those arts initiatives and policies which genuinely seek cultural democratization – not 'What are their cultures?' but 'Why are their cultures not like ours?', 'Why are their cultures not as we think they should be?'

Our starting points

Though we deal with symbolic activity and creativity in this book, we have not, therefore, found it useful to start from and write within an 'arts' perspective. The original interest at Gulbenkian (see Preface) was precisely in approaching someone from 'outside', from outside the institutions, from outside the arts world, to cast a fresh eye on the 'artistic' activities of young people. In this book we've revelled in writing from a profane, robust and independent position about issues which have become so refined and rarefied in their own temples and shrines that they sometimes cannot be identified or spoken of at all. Often they cannot be handled at all, never mind usefully or for useful purposes. But nor are we, by intention at least, anti-art or philistine in our outlook. It is simply that, in trying to argue for and present the centrality of forms of symbolic creativity in everyday 'ordinary' culture, we don't want to start from where 'art' thinks is 'here', from within its perspectives, definitions and institutions. The search for new or expanded publics has started from the wrong end of the social process – from objects and artefacts, not people.

Our 'independence', however, does not consist in simply inverting élitism. We do not pursue a cultural populism grading 'art equivalents' in popular texts – an exercise which leaves many of the definitions and forms intact whilst simply replacing the object of scrutiny, still concentrating on 'things' and finding ever more bright and clever and allusive ways of celebrating or criticizing them. Most popular cultural approaches to the 'lived' merely extend this language, this 'discourse', out from texts in a gloss and appearance of social connectedness without adding anything real to our knowledge of how symbols and forms are actually used in living cultures. In this sense popular cultural criticism and armchair semiotics have become secondhand vehicles – even when they go like Rolls-Royces – for understanding the lived. Viewing life through the glass of symbolic panels. Slumming in safety! The point for us is to try to understand the dynamic, precarious, virtual uses of symbols in common culture, not understanding the everyday through popular representation but understanding popular representation through and in the everyday. The fundamental project is to present and understand the creative symbolic elements of ordinary life, an important part of which is certainly the role and uses of popular representations, but understood through their use in – not reflection of – the everyday. The distinctiveness of this book is, then, that by ambition at least, when focusing on recognized popular cultural forms – music, fashion, the cultural media – we do so from the point of view of their use and meaning for and by young people. Our penultimate chapter focuses on everyday situations themselves, rather than on specific textual and cultural uses, and tries to show the symbolic creativity there. That is the 'centre of gravity' from which the whole book should be weighed and read, even when we are dealing with 'internal' textual or formal questions.

If you like, this is a more sociological or anthropological rather than artistic or cultural (in the sense of 'culture' as produced by or seen through texts and artefacts) starting-point, a starting-point not in clever responses to things, but in stupid responses to people. These responses are necessarily raw, open and faulted – 'stupid' – because the job is so messy and hard to do, which is why, of course, it is so rarely attempted and the 'cultural experts' stop in their chairs. Nevertheless our shared terrain with an arts or culture approach is in our central interest in symbolic creativity – though for us a sensuous and dynamic process rather than a formal feature of artistic 'things'. We argue for symbolic creativity as an integral ('ordinary') part of the human condition, not as the inanimate peaks (popular or remote) rising above its mists.

Our interest connects to a concern with a properly adequate theory of social action, of the formation and reproduction of collective and individual identities, as much as it connects to artistic or cultural concerns. To repeat, this is not to exclude 'art' from daily life, or to seek to add further social or theoretical barriers to its wider 'appreciation'. Indeed we hope to help build an altogether more satisfactory basis for thinking about the ordinary involvements of all symbolic creativity which entirely transcend tired 'appreciation' and which may lead to many innovations and new or renewed 'artistic beginnings.

All arts, dead or living, in or out of their times, can live and do live in our scheme, but they have to earn their keep. We don't wish to be in at the end of 'art' but to direct attention back to, if you like, the wellsprings of art. Our project is to establish, or re-establish, some essential, critical, uncluttered and old-fashioned truths. Creative activity, reflection and expression are in all young people's lives all of the time – only they have different names. We aim to spell out some of them.

The basic method we've used to get inside the words and to spell them out has been a loose and general form of ethnography utilizing, in particular, the recorded group discussion. We provide statistical profiles, histories and descriptive contexts where appropriate, but our main aim is to allow young people's words and experiences to come through directly into the written text. Our ethnograpic research and presentation have not aspired to a full methodological rigour, and we've ranged widely, sometimes at the cost of depth, for examples of symbolic creativity without really providing accounts of whole ways of life. But we have presented cultural items through the contexts of young people's own practices, meanings and usages of them, as gathered through our direct fieldwork methods. Discussions were taped with a variety of different groups of young people in Wolverhampton (see beginning of chapter 5 for details). These provided evidence and data which we've drawn on throughout the book; where not otherwise indicated quoted material comes usually from this source. The book also draws on a range of ethnographic fieldwork materials written up for the original Gulbenkian project (see Preface) and conducted in a variety of places including Sunderland, Leicester, South Birmingham, London and Kidderminster.

We've focused on young people, not because they are 'different', locked into some biological stage that enforces its own social condition, but simply because they provide the best and most crucial examples of our argument. The teenage and early adult years are important from a cultural perspective and in special need of a close 'qualitative' attention because it is here, at least in the first-world western cultures, where people are formed most self-consciously through their own symbolic and other activities. It is where they form symbolic moulds through which they understand themselves and their possibilities for the rest of their lives. It is also the stage where people begin to construct themselves through nuance and complexity, through difference as well as similarity.

Our main ethnographic materials are drawn from working-class experience. We have not systematically explored class differences. However, we would claim that many of the processes which we discuss hold true as tendencies in middle-class experience too, though in different and more contradictory relation to and producing different effects from school, work, the family and inherited 'cultural capital', and are major cross-class cultural levelling forces.

There are, therefore, many commonalities in youth experience and it is these we try to highlight. It is clear, however, that symbolic work and creativity can also differ in form, style and content according to age and 'life style' (living with parents or not, whether or not married, with or without children). We have not attempted to delineate this.

We have decided not to try to present a separate cultural picture of ethnic-minority youth. It is beyond our scope to do this in a properly responsible way and our focus is in any case not to provide authoritative accounts of whole cultures but to highlight the symbolic work and creativity of young people, wherever we find them. We draw many such examples from ethnic-minority experience.

Some general points, however, should be made. It is clear from our fieldwork that Caribbean and Asian traditions are very important to young black people. They use their cultural backgrounds as frameworks for living and as repertoires of symbolic resources for interpreting all aspects of their lives. This is a source of much pride to most of them and one of the fundamental means through which they explore what distinguishes them from white youth. This is necessary, not only for the development of their own identities, but also necessary as an affirmation and assertion against an omnipresent racism which tells young blacks that being 'English' means being white as well as native born, and that those who are not white can never completely fit into British culture.

But young black people can never look wholly to the prior generation for clues about how to develop their own identities. The experiences of the two generations differ, and some cultural commonalities with white youth must arise from their shared conditions of life – common experiences in the same streets and schools mediated by many of the same cultural media. Often young black people are engaged in a doubly creative task. They are trying to negotiate what it means to be a black person in a white culture at the same time as they are engaged in the same creative activities as their white peers, through which they also explore aspects of their black identities. The balance which young people strike between these things differs from culture to culture and from individual to individual.

Necessary work and symbolic creativity

Our project is to uncover, explore and present symbolic creativity in everyday life. Apart from merely asserting its importance and, we hope, demonstrating its existence, why do we insist on the visceral connection of symbolic creativity to the everyday? At bottom, what anchors it?

We argue that symbolic creativity is not only part of everyday human activity, but also a necessary part. This is because it is an integral part of *necessary work* – that which has to be done every day, that which is not extra but essential to ensure the daily production and reproduction of human existence. It is this which actually guarantees and locks in the relevance of symbolic creativity. It is this which underlies claims that the real roots of art lie in the everyday. But of what kind of necessary work do we speak? What is the basis for including symbolic creativity in it?

Necessary work is taken usually to designate the application of human capacities through the action of tools on raw materials to produce goods and services, usually through wage labour, to satisfy physical human needs. Certainly the role of symbolic creativity in this should not be underestimated. The English radical tradition[2] has stressed the dignity of labour and has sought in different ways to unify a certain view of living art with skill in work. William Morris, of course, proposed the famous general equation art = work/pleasure. Working and writing in the 1920s and 30s of this century Eric Gill[3] is perhaps the clearest, most trenchant and most recent exponent of this tradition.

For him art was the principle of skill in the making of useful things well. For him work was holy. The daily reproduction of our lives was holy. It was the play of symbolic creativity in these things which made them holy.

Unfortunately, it was evident in Gill's time, now overwhelming, that, despite the continuing human need for creativity in useful activity, modern industry has all but destroyed the possibility of 'art' in paid work. Machine production took the craft tool out of the craft hand. This more or less destroyed the possibilities of creativity at work. Automatic production takes hand, tool and body altogether out of the workplace! It is simply an idealism now to speak of 'holy' work. Nor will anyone pay the price of 'holy poverty' necessary to reintroduce 'holy work'.

But there is another kind of humanly necessary work – often

unrecognized but equally necessary – *symbolic work*. This is the application of human capacities to and through, on and with symbolic resources and raw materials (collections of signs and symbols – for instance, the language as we inherit it as well as texts, songs, films, images and artefacts of all kinds) to produce meanings. This is broader than, logically prior to and a condition of material production, but its 'necessariness' has been forgotten.

Necessary symbolic work is necessary simply because humans are communicating as well as producing beings. Perhaps they are communicative before they are productive. Whilst all may not be productive, all are communicative. *All*. This is our species distinction. Nor is this a merely formal or physiological property that might lie unused in some. Only through its exercise does communication exist and all of us communicate. This is how we manifest and produce the social and dynamic nature of our humanity.

We argue that necessary symbolic work is spread across the whole of life. It is a condition of it, and of our daily humanity. Those who stress the separateness, the sublime and quintessential in 'art' have actually assumed and encouraged a mindlessly vulgar, materialist view of everyday life. They counterpose this to their view of 'the imaginative'. They thereby view daily life as a cultural desert. The imagined symbolic deficit of everyday life is then, in its turn, to be repaired by recourse to a free-floating 'imaginative realm', to 'useless things', to 'art for art's sake', to the 'socially redundant'. But this is not only circular, it's incoherent. It's like trying to make time go faster by speeding up clocks. 'Art' is taken as the *only* field of qualitative symbolic activity, the one-per-cent transcendental value that preserves humanity. As daily life is drained of its symbolic work, 'art' is grotesquely bloated till its pores leak pure imagination. And only from 'art' can come a cultural mission into the humdrum, a doomed attempt to save the masses. Again 'art' produces culture. Symbolic work starts, not ends, in separate artefacts. The imaginative is self-validating!

We insist, against this, that imagination is not extra to daily life, something to be supplied from disembodied 'art'. It is part of the necessariness of everyday symbolic and communicative work. If declared redundant here, it will certainly not be welcomed back in the finer robes of 'art'.

This point cannot be overstated: where we can't now realistically acknowledge and promote the prospect of symbolic creativity in the sinews of necessary work as material production, we can and must recognize symbolic creativity in the sinews of necessary work as symbolic production.

What are some of the basic elements of necessary symbolic work?

First, language as a practice and symbolic resource. Language is the primary instrument that we use to communicate. It is the highest ordering of our sensuous impressions of the world, and the ultimate basis of our hope and capacity to control it. It enables interaction and solidarity with others and allows us to assess our impact on others and theirs on us. It therefore allows us to see ourselves as others.

Second, the active body as a practice and symbolic resource. The body is a site of somatic knowledge as well as a set of signs and symbols. It is the source of productive and communicative activity – signing, symbolizing, feeling.

Third, drama as a practice and symbolic resource. Communicative interaction with others is not automatic. We do not communicate from head to head through wires drilled into our skulls. Communication is achieved through roles, rituals and performances that we produce with others. Dramaturgical components of the symbolic include a variety of non-verbal communications, as well as sensuous cultural practices and communal solidarities. These include dancing, singing, joke-making, story-telling in dynamic settings and through performance.

Fourth and most importantly, symbolic creativity. Language, the body, dramatic forms are, in a way, both raw material and tools. Symbolic creativity is more fully the practice, the making – or their essence, what all practices have in common, what drives them. This is the production of *new* (however small the shift) meanings intrinsically attached to feeling, to energy, to excitement and psychic movement. This is the basis of confidence in dynamic human capacities as realities rather than as potentials – to be made conscious, through some concrete practice or active mediation, of the quality of human consciousness and how it can further be developed through the exercise and application of vital powers. Symbolic creativity can be seen as roughly equivalent to what an all-embracing and inclusive notion of the living arts might include (counterposed, of course, to the current exclusions of 'art'.) Symbolic creativity may be individual and/or collective. It transforms what is provided and helps to produce specific forms of human identity and capacity. Being human – human be-ing-ness – means to be creative in the sense of remaking the world for ourselves as we make and find our own place and identity.

What exactly is produced by symbolic work and symbolic creativity?

First, and perhaps most important, they produce and reproduce individual identities – who and what 'I am' and could become.

These may be diffuse, contradictory or decentred but they are produced through symbolic work including struggles to make meaning. Sensuous human communicative activities are also intersubjective. It is through knowing 'the other', including recognizing the self as an other for some others, that a self or selves can be known at all.

Second, symbolic work and creativity place identities in larger wholes. Identities do not stand alone above history, beyond history. They are related in time, place and things. It is symbolic work and creativity which realize the structured collectivity of individuals as well as their differences, which realize the materiality of context as well as the symbolism of self. This reminds us that locations and situations are not only *determinations* – they're also relations and resources to be discovered, explored and experienced. Memberships of race, class, gender, age and region are not only learned, they're lived and experimented with. This is so even if only by pushing up against the oppressive limits of established order and power.

Third and finally, symbolic work and especially creativity develop and affirm our active senses of our own vital capacities, the powers of the self and how they might be applied to the cultural world. This is what makes activity and identity *transitive* and specifically human. It is the dynamic and, therefore, clinching part of identity. It is the expectation of being able to apply power to the world to change it – however minutely. It is how, in the future, there is some human confidence that unities may be formed out of confusion, patterns out of irregularity. This is to be able to make judgements on who's a friend, who's an enemy, when to talk, when to hold silence, when to go, when to stop. But it's also associated with, and helps to form, overall styles of thinking which promise to make most sense of the world for you. It's also a cultural sense of what symbolic forms – languages, images, musics, haircuts, styles, clothes – 'work' most economically and creatively for the self. A culturally learned sense of the powers of the self is what makes the self in connecting it to others and to the world.

In many ways this is directly a question of cultural survival for many young people. Processes of symbolic work and symbolic creativity are very open, contested and unstable under conditions of late modernization. All young people experience one aspect or another of the contemporary 'social condition' of youth: unwilling economic dependence on parents and parental homes; uncertainty regarding future planning; powerlessness and lack of control over immediate circumstances of life; feelings of symbolic as well as material marginality to the main society; imposed institutional and ideological constructions of 'youth' which privilege certain readings and definitions of what young people should do, feel or be.[4]

Many of the traditional resources of, and inherited bases for, social meaning, membership, security and psychic certainty have lost their legitimacy for a good proportion of young people. There is no longer a sense of a 'whole culture' with allocated places and a shared, universal value system. Organized religion, the monarchy, trade unions, schools, public broadcasting, high culture and its intertwinings with public culture no longer supply ready values and models of duty and meaning to help structure the passage into settled adulthood. This is certainly partly a result of much commented-upon wider processes related to late modernization: secularization; consumerism; individualization; decollectivization; weakening respect for authority; new technologies of production and distribution. But it is also the case that these inherited traditions owe their still continuing and considerable power to the stakes they offer and seem to offer to the individual: some graspable identity within a set of relationships to other identities; some notion of citizenship within a larger whole which offers rights, satisfactions and loyalties as well as duty and submission. However, for many young people, made to feel marginal to this society, and without their own material stake in it, these merely symbolic stakes can seem very remote. These public traditions and meanings cannot make good what they offer, because they are undercut at another more basic level by unfulfilled expectations. These things are for parents and adults, for those who have an interest in and make up the civil body. For the young black British they're even more remote – they are for other people's parents. No longer can we be blind to the 'whiteness' of our major traditional public sources of identity.

Young working-class women may experience this youth condition in a special way. On the one hand they are a target consumption group for many home commodities as well as for feminine-style-and-identity products. On the other hand, and with no money recompense and no real power in the consumer market, they may be making partial, early and exploited 'transitions' (often in an imperceptible extension of childhood domestic chores 'naturally' expected of girls but not of boys) into domestic roles of care and maintenance. This may seem to be a destination of sorts and a meaningful, useful activity when labour-market opportunities are scarce or difficult, but it can often be a specific unofficial training and subjective preparation for a lifetime's future of domestic drudgery coupled with job 'opportunities' only in part-time, low-paid, insecure, usually dead-end 'female' service work.

In general the arrival of a new and extended youth stage announces itself through the arrival of new institutional forms, and the adaption of old ones, aimed at its regulation. The Youth Training Scheme, Employment Training, recent developments in youth work practice and drop-in centres for the unemployed, 'civil disorder' and community policing, changes in benefit rules for the under-25s, are all aimed in some way at controlling and filling the time of youth or at maintaining some promise (and discipline) for future transitions or at preventing and pre-empting alternative uses of time and capacity not devoted to preparation for future transitions.

There is a set of meanings and identities on offer here, highly restricted, applied and focused. They are unlikely to replace the collapsing traditional ones. Indeed the tasks of symbolic work and creativity may include not only the attempt to retain identity in the face of the erosion of traditional value systems but also to forge new resistant, resilient and independent ones to survive in and find alternatives to the impoverished roles proffered by modern state bureaucracies and rationalized industry.

Work and play

We've argued that necessary symbolic work and symbolic creativity are spread through the whole of life, through work and play. Increasingly, however, it is play that matters to this work. The informal realm of 'leisure'[5] is of vital and increasing importance for the operation of symbolic work as identity-making. There is simply decreasing room for creativity in the necessary symbolic work of most paid work,[6] so its impetus is thrown increasingly on to, or develops more in, leisure activities. A well-known sociological study of the late 1970s found that 87 per cent of a 1,000-strong sample of non-apprenticed male manual workers in Peterborough exercised more skill in driving to work than they did in work.[7] Occupational therapists seeking better opportunities for the educationally sub-normal tell us that most manual work needs only a mental age of 12 or less.[8] Perhaps that is why so many young people of more normal mental age move on restlessly, job hopping for better chances; 40 per cent of 16–24-year-olds leave their jobs every year (*General Household Survey*, 1987).

Of course, there is a whole debate concerning the changing nature of modern work with some arguing that new technology has created new and exciting opportunities for many young people. There appears to be a dominant consensus emerging,[9] however, that the workforce generally is shaping into a core/periphery pattern with a relatively large minority (the core) enjoying high pay and good security with the majority (the periphery) suffering from low pay, insecurity and high job turnover. Women, black workers and young workers constitute the main supply of peripheral labour.

Whatever the detailed arguments, the fundamental point is that most of the jobs which young people occupy simply cannot offer the intrinsic satisfaction of skill in the making of useful things well to which Eric Gill refers. There is usually no control over the task or over the use of tools and materials necessary to complete it. There is certainly no sense of the completeness of the whole work process commencing, crucially, with the human imagination of, and plans for, a desired outcome followed by the organization and use of all necessary human capacities to achieve it. The scope for symbolic work and creativity is greatly attenuated, if not destroyed. The cry for a better 'qualified' and 'skilled' workforce may well be 'new-speak', actually, for a demand for better reliability and job disci-pline amongst young workers in the face of likely (rational) responses to the mounting intrinsic meaninglessness of much modern work.

Necessary symbolic work is often now exercised not so much *through* labour, as *on* it and *about* it – using vital powers to make sense of it, comprehend its human deficits and injuries, to make and find informal alternatives and compensations.[10]

Whilst society dehumanizes work, it sentimentalizes 'Art'. So the 'arts' ignore work but are quick to condemn its 'reliefs'. But the reality is that many, if not most, young people feel more themselves in leisure than they do at work. Though only 'fun' and apparently inconsequential, it's actually where their creative symbolic abili-ties are most at play. Necessary symbolic work can operate under conditions of much greater freedom and self-energization in leisure than at work. Crucially it is the realm of the informal – specifically in the sense of freedom of symbolic activity and choice – rather than the formal. In many ways 'leisure' is now a wholly inadequate term to encompass these meanings. It simply cannot contain or invoke the sense of the massive symbolic investment now placed in free time and the ways in which it is used to explore transitional stages in growing older and to make and internalize new identities.

Informal relations certainly exist in work as a whole subter-ranean network and with their own 'unofficial' meanings. But the indirect and sometimes direct logic of capitalist production, espec-ially in the 'new competitive climate', is to press in on and try to eliminate them. Meanwhile, in an unconscious and conscious bid for cultural survival on their own terms, young people seem to turn deliberately to the informal and to resist administered symbols. It is in informal relations and informal 'free' time where they find a greater possibility of authentic and direct communication in trusting contexts. In the world of work, the managerial and public world of formal relations, people are treated like objects. Informally, it seems, people can be treated like humans, as free and equal expressive subjects. At work, sincerity, truthfulness, openness are weaknesses – things to be exploited – whereas in informal leisure these are things which seem to be valued.

In a way the spectacular sub-cultures of the 1950s and 60s prefigured some of the general shifts we are claiming for the contemporary situation. They defined themselves very early and gained their very spectacle from seeking visible identities and styles outside or against work and working respectabilities. Now the idea of a spectacular sub-culture is strictly impossible because all style and taste cultures, to some degree or another, express something of a general trend to find and make identity outside the realm of work.[11]

One way of understanding the possibilities we are arguing for in leisure is to adapt William Morris' famous equation, art = work/pleasure, by moving the terms around to produce the different formula, pleasure = art/work.[12] The realm of leisure/pleasure is not inconsequential, or 'necessary' only for the re-creation of the capacity to work in waged labour. It contains its own work, its own 'art-work', symbolic work which is about the formation and expression of identity – this work in play is more crucial in many ways than the material productions of formal worktime.

Eric Gill opens his essay 'Of slavery and freedom' with:

> That state is a state of Slavery in which a man does what he likes to do in his spare time and in his working time that which is required of him . . . That state is a state of Freedom in which a man does what he likes to do in his working time and in his spare time that which is required of him.[13]

He would, of course, have flatly rejected this notion, but it could be proposed that elements of his formulations with regard to 'leisure' have indeed come to pass. There is now a necessity in leisure, the necessary symbolic work of modern cultural survival, of developing identity and connecting its powers actively to the cultural world.

The informal and leisure agenda is much bigger now, the field for realizable emancipation much wider. The possibilities for symbolic creativity have been greatly, if contradictorily expanded. Expectations and hopes have broken free from the old suppressions to demand human significance, satisfaction, expression and development *now*. In many ways most people's lives are just being awakened after being deadened at work, boxed in, bored or worn out at home. Young people are in the vanguard of seeking pleasure, fun, autonomy and self-direction – and this quest is increasingly focused in and on leisure, in and on the hidden continent of the informal. They seek possibilities there, in their own way, which have formerly been open only in the more glamorous public worlds of artists, writers and the truly 'leisured' classes.

This is not to say that the old collective social categories have broken down under the weight of individualism and an emphasis on informal life – certainly not in an objective way. Social and cultural activities continue to be patterned and limited by class, gender and race. Often new collectivities and solidarities illuminate or are continuous with some of the aspects of the old ones. It's more that people in all groups and classes, but especially now the 'less privileged', want more and more their own 'bit of the action'. They want significance and satisfaction *now* necessarily partly as individuals and not as part of the army of other people's power. The subversion and destruction – verbally, stylistically, expressively – of stereotypical views of homogeneous class cultures is to be welcomed. For the working class this is a victory. Certain freedoms, and especially cultural ones, are felt and produce change individually. This does not signify the end of classes and groups. It is in and from these positions and mutualities, and in different ways, that individuality grows and returns to in surprising ways.

Commodities and consumerism

The main cultural materials and resources used in the symbolic work of leisure are cultural commodities. They are supplied to the market overwhelmingly by the commercial cultural industries and media for profit. Indeed it was the market discovery, exploitation and development in the 1950s and 60s of a newly defined affluent and expanding consumer group of young people which produced the popular conception of 'the teenager'.[14] We're currently experiencing a renewed and it seems even less caring emphasis on market forces in cultural matters. The rise of leisure we've referred to is really the rise of commercialized leisure. Does this matter? Does their production in a commercial nexus devalue cultural commodities and the contents of the cultural media?

There is a strange unanimity – and ghostly embrace of their opposites – between left and right when it comes to a condemnation of consumerism and especially of the penetration of the market into cultural matters. It is the profane in the Temple for the artistic establishment. For some left cultural analysts it constitutes a widened field of exploitation which is in and for itself unwelcome; now workers are exploited in their leisure as well as in their work. The circuit of domination is complete with no escape from market relations.

We disagree with both assessments, especially with their shared underlying pessimism. They both ignore the dynamic and living qualities of everyday culture and especially their necessary work and symbolic creativity. These things have always been in existence, though usually ignored or marginalized. They continue to be ignored even when an extraordinary development and transformation of them are in progress. For symbolic work and creativity mediate, and are simultaneously expanded and developed *by*, the uses, meanings and 'effects' of cultural commodities. Cultural commodities are catalyst, not product; a stage in, not the destination of, cultural affairs. Consumerism now has to be understood as an active, not a passive, process. Its play includes work.

If it ever existed at all, the old 'mass' has been culturally emancipated into popularly differentiated cultural citizens through exposure to a widened circle of commodity relations. These things have supplied a much widened range of usable symbolic resources for the development and emancipation of everyday culture. Certainly this emancipation has been partial and contradictory because the consumer industries have sought to provide some of the contents and certainly the forms as well as the possibilities for cultural activity. Consumerism continuously reproduces an image of, and therefore helps to encourage, selfishness and narcissism in individualized consumption and hedonism. But those tendencies are now given features of our cultural existence. It is the so far undervalued balance of development and emancipation which has to be grasped. As we shall see, the images and offers of consumerism are not always taken at face value, nor are 'individualized' forms of consciousness as socially isolated and self-regarding as the pessimists suppose. Meanwhile a whole continent of informal, everyday culture has been recognized, opened up and developed.

Capitalism and its images speak directly to desire for its own profit. But in that very process it breaks down or short-circuits limiting customs and taboos. It will do anything and supply any profane material in order to keep the cash tills ringing. But, in this, commerce discovered, *by exploiting*, the realm of necessary symbolic production within the undiscovered continent of the informal. No other agency has recognized this realm or supplied it with usable symbolic materials. And commercial entrepreneurship of the cultural field has discovered something real. For whatever self-serving reasons it was accomplished, we believe that this is an historical *recognition*. It counts and is irreversible. Commercial cultural forms have helped to produce an historical present from which we cannot now escape and in which there are many more materials – no matter what we think of them – available for necessary symbolic work than ever there were in the past.[15] Out of these come forms not dreamt of in the commercial imagination and certainly not in the official one – forms which make up common culture.

The hitherto hidden continent of the informal (including resources and practices drawn from traditional folk and working-class culture) produces, therefore, from cultural commodities much expounded, unprefigured and exciting effects – and this is why, of course, commerce keeps returning to the streets and common culture to find its next commodities. There is a fundamental and unstable contradictoriness in commercial rationality and instrumentality when it comes to consumer cultural goods. Blanket condemnations of market capitalism will never find room for it or understand it.

For our argument perhaps the basic complexity to be unravelled is this. Whereas it may be said that work relations and the drive for efficiency now hinge upon *the suppression* of informal symbolic work in most workers, the logic of the cultural and leisure industries hinges on the opposite tendency: a form of *their enablement and release*. Whereas the ideal model for the worker is the good time kept, the disciplined and empty head, the model for the good consumer is the converse – a head full of unbounded appetites for symbolic things.

Oddly and ironically, it is from capitalism's own order of priorities, roles, rules and instrumentalities *in production* (ironically, of leisure goods and services too) that informal cultures seek escape and alternatives in capitalist leisure *consumption*. Commerce appears twice in the cultural argument, as that which is to be escaped from and that which provides the means and materials for alternatives. Modern capitalism is now not only parasitic upon the puritan ethic, but also upon its instability and even its subversion.

There is a widespread view that these means and materials, the cultural media and cultural commodities, must appeal to the lowest common denominators of taste. Not only do they have no intrinsic value but, more disturbingly, they may have coded-in negative values which manipulate, cheapen, degrade and even brutalize the sensibilities of 'the masses'.

In contradiction we argue that there is no such thing as an autonomous artefact capable of printing its own intrinsic values, one way, on human sensibility. This is to put a ludicrous (actually crude Marxist) emphasis on *production* and what is held to be initially coded into artefacts.

What has been forgotten is that circumstances change cases, contexts change texts. The received view of aesthetics suggests that the aesthetic effect is internal to the text, and a universal property of its form. This places the creative impulse squarely on the material productions of the 'creative' artist, with the reception or consumption of art wholly determined by its aesthetic form, palely reflecting what is timelessly coded within the text. Against this we want to rehabilitate consumption, creative consumption, to see creative potentials in it for itself, rather than see it as the dying fall of the usual triplet: production, reproduction, reception. We are interested to explore how far 'meanings' and 'effects' can change quite decisively according to the social contexts of 'consumption', to different kinds of 'de-coding' and worked on by different forms of symbolic work and creativity. We want to explore how far *grounded* aesthetics are part, not of things, but of processes involving consumption, processes which make consumption pleasurable and vital. Viewers, listeners and readers do their own symbolic work on a text and create their own relationships to technical means of reproduction and transfer. There is a kind of cultural production all within consumption.

Young TV viewers, for instance, have become highly critical and literate in visual forms, plot conventions and cutting techniques. They listen, often highly selectively, to pop music now within a whole shared history of pop styles and genres. These knowledges clearly mediate the meanings of texts. The fact that many texts may be classified as intrinsically banal, contrived and formalistic must be put against the possibility that their living reception is the opposite of these things.

The 'productive' reception of and work on texts and artefacts can also be the start of a social process which results in its own more concrete productions, either of new forms or of recombined existing ones. Perhaps we should see the 'raw materials' of cultural life, of communications and expressions, as always intermediate. They are the products of one process as well as the raw materials for another, whose results can be, in turn, raw materials for successive groups. Why shouldn't bedroom decoration and personal styles, combinations of others' 'productions', be viewed along with creative writing or song and music composition as fields of aesthetic realization? Furthermore the grounded appropriation of new technology and new hardware may open new possibilities for expression, or recombinations of old ones, which the dominant culture misses because it does not share the same conditions and contradictory pressures of that which is to be explained or come to terms with.

Our basic point is that human consumption does not simply repeat the relations of production – and whatever cynical motives lie behind them. Interpretation, symbolic action and creativity are *part* of consumption. They're involved in the whole realm of necessary symbolic work. This work is at least as important as whatever might originally be encoded in commodities and can often produce their opposites. Indeed some aspects of 'profanity' in commercial artefacts may be liberating and progressive, introducing the possibility of the new and the socially dynamic.

It is pointless and limiting to judge artefacts *alone*, outside their social relations of consumption, with only the tutored critic's opinion of an internal aesthetic allowed to count. This is what limits the 'Official Arts' in their institutions. People bring living identities to commerce and the consumption of cultural commodities as well as being formed there. They bring experiences, feelings, social position and social memberships to their encounter with commerce. Hence they bring a necessary creative symbolic pressure, not only to make sense of cultural commodities, but partly through them also to make sense of contradiction and structure as they experience them in school, college, production, neighbourhood, and as members of certain genders, races, classes and ages. The results of this necessary symbolic work may be quite different from anything initially coded into cultural commodities.

Grounded aesthetics

As we have used the term so far, 'symbolic creativity' is an abstract concept designating a human capacity almost in general. It only exists, however, in contexts and, in particular, sensuous living processes. To identify the particular dynamic of symbolic activity and transformation in concrete named situations we propose the term 'grounded aesthetic'. This is the creative element in a process whereby meanings are attributed to symbols and practices and where symbols and practices are selected, reselected, highlighted and recomposed to resonate further appropriated and particularized meanings. Such dynamics are emotional as well as cognitive. There are as many aesthetics as there are grounds for them to operate in. Grounded aesthetics are the yeast of common culture.

We have deliberately used the term 'aesthetic' to show both the differences and the continuities of what we are trying to say with respect to the culture and arts debate. We are certainly concerned with what might be called principles of beauty, but as qualities of living symbolic activities rather than as qualities of things; as ordinary aspects of common culture, rather than as extraordinary aspects of uncommon culture. This is the sense of our clumsy but strictly accurate use of 'grounded'.

Our 'groundedness' for some will seem simply no more than the reckless destruction of flight, potting birds of paradise with sociological lead. For others the strange search for archaic aesthetics in grounded, everyday social relations will seem perverse, un-material and even mystical. We're happy to work on the assumption that 'the truth' lies somewhere, always provisionally, in between, that human be-ing-ness needs both air and earth and, in turn, makes possible our very idea of both.

Within the process of creating meanings from and within the use of symbols there may be a privileged role for texts and artefacts, but a grounded aesthetic can also be an element and a quality of everyday social relations. For instance, there is a dramaturgy and poetics of everyday life, of social presence, encounter and event. It may have become invisible in the routinized roles of adult life, but the young have much more time and they face each other with fewer or more fragile masks. They are the practical existentialists. They sometimes have no choice but to be, often too, absorbed in the moment and to ransack immediate experience for grounded aesthetics. For them some features of social life may not be about the regulation and containment of tension, but about its creation and increase. The 'aimless' life of groups and gangs may be about producing something from nothing, from 'doing nothing'. It may be about building tensions, shaping grounded aesthetics, orchestrating and shaping their release and further build-ups, so that a final 'catharsis' takes with it or changes other tensions and stresses inherent in the difficulties of their condition. Making a pattern in an induced swirl of events can produce strangely still centres of heightened awareness where time is held and unusual control and insight are possible. Grounded aesthetics are what lift and mark such moments.

Grounded aesthetics are the specifically creative and dynamic moments of a whole process of cultural life, of cultural birth and rebirth. To know the cultural world, our relationship to it, and ultimately to know ourselves, it is necessary not merely to be in it but to change – however minutely – that cultural world. This is a making specific – in relation to the social group or individual and its conditions of life – of the ways in which the received natural and social world is made human *to them* and made, to however small a degree (even if finally symbolic), controllable by them.

The possibility of such control is, of course, a collective principle for the possibility of political action on the largest scale. But it also has importance in the individual and collective awareness of the ability to control symbols and their cultural work. Grounded aesthetics produce an edge of meaning which not only reflects or repeats what exists, but transforms what exists – received expressions and appropriated symbols as well as what they represent or are made to represent in some identifiable way.

In so called 'primitive art' and culture, for instance, a central theme is the naming of fundamental forces as gods and demons, thereby to reveal them, make them somehow knowable and therefore subject to human persuasion or placation. Of course, the urban industrial world is much more complex in its organization than are 'primitive' societies, and our apparent technical control over the threatening forces of nature seems greater and different in kind from theirs. What we seek to control, persuade or humanize through grounded aesthetics may be, in part, the force and expression of other human beings rather than forces emanating directly from nature – if you like the work of culture on culture.

A sense of or desire for timelessness and universality may be part of the impulse of a grounded aesthetic. The natural, obvious and immutable become particular historical constructions capable of variation. Subjectivity, taken to some degree out of the particular, is the force which can change it. But we may equally focus on the particular extracted from its context to make sense of the universal (Blake's grain of sand). Such psychic separation may be part of and/or a condition for some grounded aesthetics.

This is not to say that 'universals' really exist, certainly not internally in 'art-objects'. It is extraordinary how many universals – and contradictory ones – are claimed. Nevertheless, experienced universalism, as a movement out of or reperception of the particular, may well be a universal feature of heightened human awareness. This universalism is also a kind of awareness of the future in terms of what it is possible to become. This is part of heightened aspiration and the quest for wider significance and expanded identity. Universalism also gives some vision of the kind of socialness and human mutuality which might locate better and more expanded identities. Grounded aesthetics provide a motivation towards realizing different futures, and for being in touch with the self as a dynamic and creative force for bringing them about.

The received sense of the 'aesthetic' emphasizes the cerebral, abstract or sublimated quality of beauty. At times it seems to verge on the 'an-aesthetic' – the suppression of all senses. By contrast we see grounded aesthetics as working through the senses, through sensual heightening, through joy, pleasure and desire, through 'fun' and the 'festive'.

Concrete skills, concretely acquired rather than given through natural distinction or gift, are involved in the exercise of grounded aesthetics. 'Economy', and 'skill', for instance, enter into the grounded aesthetics of how the body is used as a medium of expression. A bodily grounded aesthetic enters into personal style and presence, dance and large areas of music and performance.

Although they are not things, grounded aesthetics certainly have uses. Such uses concern the energizing, developing and focusing of vital human powers on to the world in concrete and practical ways, but also in lived connected cognitive ways. This is in producing meanings, explanations and pay-offs in relation to concrete conditions and situations which seem more efficient or adequate than other proffered official or conventional meanings. Such 'useful' meanings may well have moral dimensions in providing collective and personal principles of action, co-operation, solidarity, distinction or resistance.

But 'useful' meanings can also be very private. There are perhaps especially private, symbolic and expressive therapies for the injuries of life. They 'work', not through their direct musical, literary or philosophical forms, but through the ways in which a grounded aesthetic produces meanings and understandings which were not there before. This may involve internal, imaginative and spiritual life. It may be in the realm of dream and fantasy, in the realm of heightened awareness of the constructedness and constructiveness of the self: alienation from obvious givens and values; the sense of a future made in the present changing the present; the fear of and fascination for the 'terra incognita' of the self. The usefulness of grounded aesthetics here may be in the holding and repairing, through some meaning creation and human control even in desperate seas, of the precariousness and fragmentedness of identity whose source of disturbance is outside, structural and beyond the practical scope of individuals to influence.

The crucial failure and danger of most cultural analysis are that dynamic, living grounded aesthetics are transformed and transferred into ontological properties of things, objects and artefacts which may represent and sustain aesthetics but which are, in fact, separate. The aesthetic effect is not *in* the text or artefact. It is part of the sensuous/emotive/cognitive creativities of human receivers, especially as they produce a stronger sense of emotional and cognitive identity as expanded capacity and power – even if only in the possibility of *future* recognitions of a similar kind. These creativities are not dependent on texts, but might be enabled by them.[16]

Surprising meanings and creativities can be generated from un-
promising materials through grounded aesthetics. But texts and
artefacts can also fail to mediate symbolic meanings for many
reasons. Many supply only a narrow or inappropriate (for particular
audiences) range of symbolic resources. Others encourage *reification* (literally, making into a thing) rather than the *mediation* and
enablement of the possibility of grounded aesthetics. They move
too quickly to supply a putative aesthetic. The receivers are simply
sent a 'message', the meaning of which is pre-formed and pre-given.
Signs are pinned succinctly and securely to their meanings. Human
receivers are allowed no creative life of their own. The attempt to
encapsulate directly an aesthetic militates against the possibility of
its realization through a grounded aesthetic because the space for
symbolic work of reception has been written out.

There are many ways in which the 'official arts' are removed from
the possibility of a living symbolic *mediation*, even despite their
possible symbolic richness and range. Most of them are out of their
time and, even though this should enforce no veto on current
mediation, the possibilities of a relevant structuring of symbolic
interest are obviously limited. The institutions and practices
which support 'art', however, seem designed to break any living
links or possibilities of inducing a grounded aesthetic appropriation. 'Official' art equates aesthetics with artefacts. In literature,
for instance, all of our current social sense is read *into* the text as its
'close reading' – the legacy of deadness left by I. A. Richards and
F. R. Leavis. Art objects are put into the quietness and stillness of
separate institutions – which might preserve them, but not their
relation to the exigencies of current necessary symbolic work. The
past as museum, Art as objects! The reverence and distance encouraged by formality, by institutions, and by the rites of liberal-
humanist education as 'learning the code', kill dead, for the vast
majority, what the internal life of signs might offer through
grounded aesthetics to current sensibility and social practice. It is
as hard for the 'official arts' to offer themselves to grounded aesthetics, as it is for grounded aesthetics to find recognition in the formal
canons.

Commercial cultural commodities, conversely, offer no such
impediments. At least cultural commodities – for their own bad
reasons – are aimed at exchange and therefore at the possibility of
use. In responding to, and attempting to exploit, current desires and
needs, they are virtually guaranteed to offer some relevance to the
tasks of current socially necessary symbolic work. In crucial
senses, too, the modern media precisely 'mediate' in passing back
to audiences, at least in the first instance, symbolic wholes they've

taken from the streets, dance-halls and everyday life. Along with this they may also take, however imperfectly and crudely, a field of aesthetic tensions from daily life and from the play of grounded aesthetics there.

Of course, part of the same restless process is that cultural commodities, especially style and fashion 'top end down', may become subject overwhelmingly to reification, symbolic rationalization and the drastic reduction of the symbolic resources on offer. But consumers move too. When cultural commodities no longer offer symbolic mediation to grounded aesthetics, they fall 'out of fashion'. And in the cumulative symbolic landscape of consumer capitalism, dead packaged, reified grounded aesthetics are turned back into primary raw material for other processes of inevitable necessary symbolic work, with only the cultural theorists paranoically labouring back along their 'meta-symbolic' routes to 'golden age' symbolic homologies. This commercial process may, to say the least, be flawed, but it offers much more to grounded aesthetics than do the dead 'offical arts'.

There may well be a better way, a better way to cultural emancipation than through this continuous instability and trust in the hidden – selfish, blind, grabbing – hand of the market. But 'official art' has not shown it yet. Commercial cultural commodities are all most people have. History may be progressing through its bad side. But it progresses. For all its manifest absurdities, the cultural market may open up the way *to* a better way. We have to make our conditions of life before we can dominate and use them. Cultural pessimism offers us only road-blocks.

Against post-modernist pessimism

The much commented upon incandescence – instability, changeability, luminosity – of cultural commodities ('all that is solid melts into air'[17]) is not some form of spontaneous combustion in commodities or another 'wonder' of capitalist production. It is not without or against meaning. This very incandescence passes through *necessary symbolic work*, changes and enables it. The incandescence is not simply a surface market quality. It produces, is driven by, and reproduces further forms and varieties for everyday symbolic work and creativity, some of which remain in the everyday and in common culture far longer than they do on the market.

The market is the source of a permanent and contradictory revolution in everyday culture which sweeps away old limits and dependencies. The markets' restless search to find and make new appetites raises, wholesale, the popular currency of symbolic aspiration. The currency may be debased and inflationary, but aspirations now circulate, just as do commodities. That circulation irrevocably makes or finds its own new worlds.

The style and media theorists – and terrorists – of the left and right see only market incandescence. They warn us of an immanent semiotic implosion of all that is real. They call us to a strange rejection of all that glitters and shimmers over the dark landscape, as if it *were* the landscape. But this usually metropolitan neurosis is nothing more than a bad case of idealist theorists' becoming the victims of their own nightmares. Mistaking their own metaphors for reality, they are hoist by their own semiotic petards. They are caught by – defined in professionally charting – the symbolic life on the surface of things without seeing, because not implicated in, the *necessary* everyday role of symbolic work, of how sense is made of structure and contradiction. They then coolly announce that modern culture is all surface in danger of collapse.

We must catch up with the movement of the real world. We must not be satisfied with a phantom history and demonology of its surface movement. Above all, self-deluding and complacent beliefs in aesthetic self-sufficiency and separateness, as sanctuaries in and against an imaginary history, must be firmly rejected.

Commerce and consumerism have helped to release a profane explosion of everyday symbolic life and activity. The genie of common culture is out of the bottle – let out by commercial carelessness. Not stuffing it back in, but seeing what wishes may be granted, should be the stuff of our imagination.

Notes

1 Raymond Williams, 'Culture is ordinary' (1958), reprinted in his *Resources of Hope*, Verso, 1988.

2 We are thinking of the line that runs through from Cobbett, Blake, Ruskin and William Morris.

3 See, for instance, *A Holy Tradition of Working*, Golgonooza Press, 1983.

4 For a full account of the 'new social condition of youth' in relation to youth unemployment, see P. Willis *et al.*, *The Youth Review*, Avebury, 1988.

5 'Leisure' is a difficult term which only roughly indicates our intended meaning. We use it only because of the lack of well-known or meaningful alternatives. Problems with the term include the way it can be extended to cover the oppressions of unemployment by calling it 'free time'; the inadequacy of framing women's informal creativity as 'leisure' when the home more even than paid

labour is a site of repetitive and boring work for them and when their freedom to move out of doors is curtailed by violence and the fear of violence; most importantly, the inconsequential and optional nature of what is usually meant by 'leisure'.

6 The following discussion of the symbolic components of work is necessarily rather truncated. It refers only to symbolic activity in relation to the *intrinsic* or *official* elements of deskilled modern work. Though it is not our direct focus here, we would certainly not deny that work continues to be an important *general* and interlinked site of cultural experience. Cultures of work are varied, contradictory, inner and outer related, and have to be carefully dissected. There continues to be an unofficial richness in work relations which is directed against the coercion or bankruptcy of its official requirements. This links outwards to effect forms of free-time informality and intimacy, but unofficial work cultures also fully utilize and attempt to make space for many of the forms, interests and communications of 'leisure' and 'free time'. Work continues to be where many people spend most of their time, where they find their main social contacts and where their and their dependents' living and leisuring are earned. These are all crucial relationships to be made sense of at a cultural level (both in and out of work), even if leisure and informal rather than 'shop floor' resources are increasingly used for this sense-making. The study of this needs, and must await, another book.

7 R. Blackburn and M. Mann, *The Working Class in the Labour Market*, Macmillan, 1979.

8 P. Willis, *Learning to Labour*, Gower, 1977.

9 See, for instance, a recent summary reviewed in the *Financial Times* (24 August 1989), A. Lindbeck and D. J. Snomer, *The Insider–Outsider Theory of Employment and Unemployment*, MIT, 1989.

10 None of this amounts to welcoming or justifying mass unemployment. All studies show that the vast majority of young people find almost any kind of work preferable to unemployment. However, this tells us more about the extreme negative qualities of work-lessness – poverty, total boredom, exclusion from 'leisure' and consumption, isolation, depression – than it does about any positive quality in work.

11 A point first made and developed in a working summary paper by Geoff Hurd.

12 This was suggested by Stephen Yeo in conversation.

13 *A Holy Tradition of Work*, op. cit, page 97.

14 See the first major study of youth culture in Britain, Mark Abrams, *The Teenage Consumer*, London Press Exchange, 1959.

15 We're bending the stick of argument here to emphasize how cultural products are creatively *used*, rather than passively *consumed*. We should not, of course, ignore the continuing ubiquity of forms of direct cultural production such as writing, photography and 'storying' (c.f. D. Morley and K. Worpole, *The Republic of Letters*, Comedia, 1981; S. Beszceret and P. Corrigan, *Towards a Different Image*, Comedia/Methuen, 1986; S. Yeo, *Whose Story?*, Blackwell, 1990). Equally, against élitism, we should recall activities like knitting and gardening as combining both production and use. Our general argument here should not obscure that varieties of such 'home produce' are important fields for symbolic work and creativity.

16 It is possible to get into a fine and tautological argument about the distinctions and relationships between 'invisible' internal subjective meanings and external 'visible' signs, symbols and practices. Though we insist that grounded aesthetics are a quality of living processes of meaning-making, not of things, this is not necessarily a wholly invisible internal process, though it can be. Words, signs, symbols and practices as 'things' in the world can certainly be part of the operation of particular grounded aesthetics for particular people. They are also taken in by and made sense of in the meaning-making of others. Also we recognize and, in what follows, give many examples of the possibility of grounded aesthetics becoming properly externalized: formalized, made concrete and public in some way. We argue for this as a process which decisively blurs and questions the conventional distinctions between consumption and production. What's crucial here, though, is not the 'thing-like' qualities of such externalizations, but their capacity both to reflect *and promote* the grounded aesthetics of their producers and of others, individuals and collectivities.

Our internal subjective meanings will never transcend or make redundant the 'given-ness' of textuality, of things, of forms, of symbols. Indeed these latter are intrinsic to the possibility and creativity of human meanings, but they should always be seen transitively for their role in the mediation of human meaning. They're humble, malleable things, not the kings and queens of expression and experience. In particular, we should understand that processes of human meaning-making and creativity are stopped dead when aesthetics are attached to things instead of to human activities.

17 The title of a book by Marshall Berman (Simon and Schuster, New York, 1982) which helped to launch the many faceted and pervasive post-modern debate.

The cultural media and symbolic creativity

The omnipresent cultural media of the electronic age provide a wide range of symbolic resources for, and are a powerful stimulant of, the symbolic work and creativity of young people. The media help to mediate the new possibilities of common culture. Time and again in our research we were brought back to the pervasiveness of the cultural media in youth experience. The media enter into virtually all of their very creative activities. But whilst the media invite certain interpretations, young people have not only learnt the codes, but have learnt to play with interpreting the codes, to reshape forms, to interrelate the media through their own grounded aesthetics. They add to and develop new meanings from given ones. The young are the most sophisticated 'readers' of images and media of any group in society. The meanings they derive from these things inform all their activities. Most importantly the cultural media are used as a means to vitality, to provide and construct dimensions for what they are and might become.

Television

All the evidence we have suggests that television is a major force in the organization of young people's leisure and pleasure, not only in terms of the time actually spent in front of the screen but also through its connections with other cultural activities. For some pastimes television offers a convenient substitute. Although the great majority of regular cinema-goers are concentrated in the 15–24 age range, for example, studies reveal some young people prefer to watch films on video or off air. In other areas, however, the small screen acts as powerful stimulus to activity by helping to focus attention on particular leisure options and products. Books based around television shows regularly make the best-seller lists.

The television coverage of sports new to Britain, such as American football, helps to create new constituencies of fans and amateur players. The promotional videos that form the backbone of much 'youth' programming are now an essential tool in launching records in the mainstream rock and pop markets. Finally television itself – its stars, scandals and behind-the-scenes bust-ups – has become a major topic of public interest and attention, with stories of television personalities and soap-opera stars often edging politicians off the tabloid front pages.

Television, in short, has become a pervasive part of the cultural and symbolic life of young people in its widest sense.

What exactly is television? Ten years ago this would have seemed a ridiculous question. Television was synonymous with what broadcasters provided. Everything that appeared on the domestic screen was produced, purchased and presented either by the BBC or by one of the independent television (ITV) companies. From around 1982, however, this situation changed. New industries offering new channels and other ways to use the small screen began to gather momentum. The first wave centred around video cassette recorders (VCRs) and home computers, to be joined in the late 1980s by the arrival of direct-to-home satellite broadcasting and the growth of new broadband local cable systems, both of which add a range of new channels to those provided by the BBC and ITV. To talk of television in today's context, then, is to talk of a series of institutions and industries, each offering a particular mixture of opportunities and options for use.

Surveys of young people's spare time show that along with listening to the radio and playing records and tapes, watching television is far and away the most universal leisure activity. The peak periods for watching are either side of the times when young people are most likely to be out of the house; the early evening (between 5 p.m. and 7 p.m.) and the late evening. Though going out doesn't necessarily mean no television. Pubs, for example, often have sets behind the bar, or sets tuned to one of the new satellite-delivered stations such as the rock-music channel, MTV.

The pervasiveness of television in young people's lives has prompted a range of worries about its ill effects. Much of this commentary is based on a view of the youthful audience as passive, uncreative recipients of 'messages' that enter their consciousness from outside – like a drug injected into a vein – causing altered behaviour and thinking. This view, however, is comprehensively contradicted by a range of recent research that has tried to observe people watching television in their own homes rather than in a laboratory, and has talked to them at length about their feelings and responses, allowing them to speak in their own voice, without reducing their answers to ticks on a predesigned questionnaire.

The study conducted by Peter Collet of Oxford University which filmed people watching television and recorded their comments using equipment concealed in the television cabinet, provides a particularly revealing picture of everyday viewing. The tapes showed that people have their eyes on the screen for only two-thirds of the time they are in the room. The rest of the time they are reading the newspaper, dozing, and doing a variety of other things. And, when they are watching, they are far from passive. They shout back at the screen, make sarcastic comments about people's hair-styles and dress sense, sing along with the advertising jingles, talk about the programmes while they are still on. Far from being the passive watchers of political mythology, they actively collaborate with the screen to create and recreate a web of meanings that are relevant to them and anchored in their own lives. They develop active and varied relationships with the TV screen and creatively and selectively take up its meanings and messages into their own symbolic work. They develop their own grounded aesthetics in forms of creative consumption.

From our Wolverhampton fieldwork it is clear that TV is an omnipresent part of daily life: 'Whether we're watching or not, it's buzzing in the background'; 'It's just more homely when I have it on in the kitchen'. It can also be a foreground: 'You tend to be able to make good conversation out of it'. But there are no 'automatic effects' from the TV on young people's lives or perceptions. Young people, especially, actively control where and how TV functions in their own landscape. They are highly 'TV literate' in interpreting sounds and images and taking them up into their own grounded symbolic work and meanings.

Amongst our respondents we found a widespread understanding of television as an institution and as a cultural producer operating under its own symbolic and material conditions and restrictions, not least in the context of the profit/audience-driven ratings war:

> RACHEL: Sometimes, say, you've got too many characters, that would ruin the story. It's like, you've got one black middle-class family, you've got one that's – um – way up on the top, then you've got one on the breadline. If it's like that, if you've got all stages of people, there would be too many characters. Because the less characters there are, the more you can concentrate on the people and bring out their character, and bring out the story . . .

SANDRA: They only have bad black people to build up the ratings.

There is a widespread familiarity with and understanding of different conventions, stereotypes and TV genres: 'Comedy ain't meant to be realistic, it's meant to make you laugh'; '*EastEnders*, you know what to expect before it happens'; 'They portray black women to be big, big busted and big butts and fat'; 'Excitement, money . . . getting involved in the quizzes and questions they ask, guessing the answer before they say'; 'American soaps exaggerate the good points and ours exaggerate the bad points'. As these quotes show, there is a grounded aesthetic in simply identifying how the different conventions invite you to play a role and in deciding how to respond to them – far from a passive activity, even if someone else is defining the roles.

It is true that most television was judged in our discussion groups by criteria relating to realism. But this does not imply interpretive laziness or vulnerability to realist 'ideologies'. The exercise of realist criteria requires the active work of comparison and, ironically and contradictorily, a full working knowledge of the difference between reality and representation. This is precisely about a grounded fictive aesthetic which can separate and recombine representation and reality. They do not mistake fiction for reality. Rather the reverse, they understand that it's the reality behind how the shows are made which helps to determine their form and quality as 'realistic' representations:

JC: Do you like *Dallas*?

SANDRA: I liked it at the beginning, but then I think it went down a bit. I think it went down since it came back. The part that ruined it was when, um, Pam, was having that dream about how Bobby got killed or something like that, I think it got ruined then.

MARGARET: It was a bit stupid . . . fantasy. But they had to do that because these top actors, right, they decided they were gonna quit the place, the film, and when they got offered more money, they got back into it.

Nor is the realist template standardized or without distinctions. Comparative tastes are clear and evaluative criteria well developed, expressed often through ridicule and a practical 'deconstructionist' eye for breaking down the 'reality effect':

KATY: My husband likes the 'Carry On' films and oh, God, I mean, I've watched every one about three times, but he can watch them over and over again. When one comes on I always say 'You're not gonna watch this, I'm sick to death of them. You know exactly what's gonna happen next.' I like love stories [laughs]. He'll watch them, but you know, he'll sit there taking the mickey.

LIAL: I have to watch it [*Neighbours*]. My girlfriend watches it and it's, ugh . . . I don't like soaps, they're boring. It's like they've got five houses and everything happens in those five houses. Abortions, people getting killed, dope, beating up, everything in those five houses! Not that much goes on around here! Too blown up and a waste of time!

Despite this last quote, soap operas rather than programmed youth material were generally the most favoured TV forms in our discussion groups. Soaps provide materials towards many possible interpretations and counter-identifications. They accept different readings and set up clear spaces for the symbolic work and active participation of different viewers. The realist orientation of evaluation amongst the young people we spoke to does not mean the more realism the better for them. Rather there was a varying but intricate balance of taste quoted time and again between the appreciation of a realistic portrayal of a recognizable reality and an interest in glamour and the 'larger than life'. The importance of programmes connecting in some way to life as it is actually lived emerges very strongly from the way young women talked about soap operas,

the soaps they're more down to earth, I'm not being funny, but it's like the American soaps what are glamorous, 'cause I mean, look at *Brookside* . . . Just normal people . . . But *Dallas* and all that, they seem to like exaggerate everything, so lovely, and they're made of money. It's just something you watch to get out of life for a bit . . . But like *EastEnders* and *Brookside* you can't forget about the world.

Although American soaps were enjoyed as a way to 'forget about your world for a bit' the immense popularity of the British shows rested on the way they explored problems and situations that young women could imagine themselves facing in a way that combined believability with drama and a dash of glamour. *Coronation Street* was disliked by some for getting this balance wrong:

Coronation Street, I watch it, but I can't say that I really look forward to it, I mean, we always have it on, think it's routine, but I think it's a bit dreary really . . . I think it's just, I don't think anything exciting happens really in it. There isn't, you know . . . perhaps that's even more true to life. I think you want to get away from it a bit [laughs]. It's mainly the pub, isn't it, I think nothing really happens in it and perhaps the people haven't got any glamour either.

By the same token, *EastEnders* was criticized for going overboard on drama,

they tried to smack everything in, like Michelle had the abortion, and Den knocking her off. You know what I mean, and they spoilt it really, they've got no story to it now, it's just boring. They've done all the story lines.

The variable relation between reality and representation and the very exaggeration of many soaps seemed to provide some important inputs towards a particular kind of informal symbolic work. This concerned the development of extended and contexted evaluative moral criteria for judging and assessing a whole range of real-life situations which involve or might involve young people:

JC: What kinds of things are you learning [from the soaps]?
SANDRA: Not to borrow money from the loan shark, 'cause Arthur was having a nervous breakdown and he started borrowing money and that.
RACHEL: He's a fool.
MARGARET: And not to mix with the wrong kind of people.
SANDRA: Yeah, like drugs as well . . . Like Mary, she's a one . . . she's a single parent. But she's a prostitute, she's taking drugs now, which will be interesting to see. And Wixy, he's gonna catch AIDS the way he's carrying on.
RACHEL: Why?
SANDRA: . . . he has a girl every single night, and I mean, he, he's just disgusting, he's so slack.
JC: Do you think that it's typical that a single mother that's on the dole becomes a –
SANDRA: If she's really desperate.
RACHEL: It depends. She can be on the dole, have a child, but still live at home.
MARGARET: Depends on how she's been brought up. If she had a lot of freedom.
RACHEL: Because I know somebody who's a one-parent family and she, she ain't nothin' like that, nothin' at all.
SANDRA: It depends. If you ain't got no family or anything, and you live in a really bad flat, then they might decide to be a prostitute. For that only purpose.

Altogether there is clearly a fine line between representation and reality. Reality itself depends on and is in part constituted by representation, of images, arguments, moralities. But it is precisely the fine practical knowledge of this fine line which gives enjoyment – 'the pleasure of the text' – in the symbolic work and creativity of crossing and recrossing it, extending the fiction sometimes for yourself as well as deciding to take fiction as real for some purposes. A grounded aesthetic in viewing TV and in our discussion groups was precisely about this playfulness, not about realism as an absolute or as an expectation and assumption of 'truth' in images.

MARGARET: . . . then you want to see what happens next week, so you keep on carrying on watching it.
SHARMA: That's it.
JC: Do you talk with your friends about these shows?
SEVERAL: Yeah . . .
MARGARET: You watch it 'cause there's nothing else on the telly.
RACHEL: When you watch the show, you don't really think like that. You just watch it for the enjoyment of it . . . you don't really think that people live like that.
SHARMA: You like to predict it, don't you? Think of what's going to happen next.
SANDRA: In *EastEnders*, I think some people are like that. Dirty Den . . .

YVONNE: Sometimes it [*EastEnders*] is [boring]. Yes, sometimes there isn't any story line. It's just like ordinary.
JO: The same, innit? Go to the pub for a drink, Pauline and Arthur! . . . Arthur's nicked some margarine from the store where he's been working and Pauline's going and the Gran's going um, um, um [laughs] . . .
ANGELA: That Gran gets on my nerves.
JO: Michelle's frowning all the time. Moan, moan. She's a right mard that woman is. She's never happy.

From the external vantage point of many critics and commentators soap operas are easily dismissed as wall-to-wall trivia, undemanding entertainment. But as our quotes show, the young women who watch them are constantly judging them and reworking the material they provide, finding echoes in their own lives and spaces which allow them to ask what would happen 'if'. TV watching is, at least in part, about facilitating a dialectic between representation and reality as a general contribution to symbolic work and creativity. The audience is not an empty room waiting to be furnished in someone else's taste.

The fact that young people have an active, creative, and symbolically productive relation to what they see on television does not mean that what is provided has no 'effects'. But we need to find new ways of thinking about this familiar issue. 'Effects' are the result, not of TV programmes, but of the whole creative relation of viewers with what they see. More symbolic resources supplied through the TV screen would certainly enhance that relationship but not as a mechanical causation with measurable 'effects'. Instead of concentrating solely on the impact of particular programmes and of areas of content, such as violence, we should more properly consider what is missing or disappearing from the current schedules. The scope for creative engagement with television depends in large part on the available range of programming and the diversity of youth experience reflected within it. The aim must always be to increase the range of usable symbolic resources available for symbolic work.

The central problem with the broadcasting system we have at the moment is that it operates with a relatively narrow and impoverished conception of 'youth'. Specific youth programming too often predigests and completes, too early and on behalf of the viewer, the work of symbolic meaning and sense-making – that which it's implied or assumed the young viewer is incapable of or needs help in. This assumption of youth symbolic laziness, or in some cases imbecility, is responsible in part for the development of two clear poles in the treatment of youth issues on TV – youth as 'fun', youth as 'trouble': *Blind Date* or *Panorama*. Fun or concern is forced down the viewer's TV throat rather than left to be an open result of the viewer's exercise of taste, discrimination and capacity for symbolic work.

The central aim for future policy must be to work for a programme system that offers the maximum diversity of information, experience, argument and analysis relevant to the lives and concerns of young people. This means two things. First, a commitment to represent the full variety of youth experience in the general run of programming, from soap operas and drama series to situation comedies, news and documentaries. Second, a variety of programmes directed specifically at young people using a range of styles and formats that allows the diversity of youth experience to be engaged with in a number of different ways and which provides opportunities for young people to speak and represent themselves in their own voice and style. The resulting mix would include not only rock music and fashion programmes, but access programmes made in collaboration with young people, studio-based shows giving young people a chance to question politicians, show-business personalities and others, and programmes which allow them to voice their criticisms of broadcasting itself. All these kinds of programmes already exist. The question is whether they will continue to exist and develop in the new deregulated television environment.

Video recorders and cable

Over the last five years, the video cassette recorder (VCR) has become a familiar extension to the television set in many homes. By 1987, 68 per cent of 16–24-year-olds in the United Kingdom were living in households with a machine. Despite the frequently voiced claim that we are living through a 'video revolution', the available evidence shows that VCRs are mainly used to record and play back broadcast programmes which are on at an awkward time or which clash with something else people want to see. According to a recent survey conducted by the Independent Broadcasting Authority (IBA), almost three-quarters (74 per cent) of VCR users claimed to view television programmes they had recorded at least once a week. The ability to time-shift programmes is video's main attraction, since it allows people to construct their own evening's viewing, watching what they want when they want. As one young Wolverhampton couple explain:

> On an evening, the programmes we like, well we usually go from one soap to another. We watch *Brookside*, *Emmerdale Farm*, *Top of the Pops*, *EastEnders*. Like last night we watched *EastEnders* and taped *Auf Wiedersehen Pet*, on the other side, and then we watched *The Bill*, which is a police serial. Then we watched *Auf Wiedersehen Pet*, which was off the video.

Overall though, recent surveys show that the total time people in Britain spend playing back recorded material has dropped significantly, from 6.07 hours at the beginning of 1986 to 4.38 hours by the middle of 1988, suggesting that some of the early novelty has now worn off.

Although only 30 per cent of users overall watch films they have hired from their local shop on their VCRs, this is a relatively popular activity among young people. This is scarcely surprising since the 16–24 age group has always been the primary audience of new films, with 40 per cent of those taking part in a 1987 national survey claiming to go once every three months or more as against only 15 per cent of 25–34-year-olds and 6 per cent of 35–64-year-olds.[1] Contrary to the impression created by the panic over 'video nasties' and the continuing concern over what young people are watching on their VCRs, surveys of tape rentals show that the range of films borrowed is much the same as the mix of films shown on the major cinema circuits, with comedies, thrillers and horror films proving easily the most popular. Pornography is a very small part of the overall rental market and its share has been dropping steadily, from 4 per cent in 1985 to 2 per cent in 1988.

In the last couple of years sales of prerecorded tapes have begun to gather momentum as prices have come down and a wider range of material has been released. Among 16–24-year-olds this market is centred solidly around videos of rock and pop stars.

However, this does not mean that video is simply an extension of the television set or the cinema auditorium. It also has unique characteristics which change the nature of viewing in important ways. By releasing people from the preset schedules of the broadcasters and cinema managers it can make viewing a different kind of social experience as people gather in one another's houses to watch a new film or rock video release. It also gives viewers more control over the way they watch and over the materials of their own symbolic work. They can speed-scan the whole thing, skip sequences they don't like, repeat ones they do, slow the action down, and freeze a single frame on the screen. By allowing a more active relationship to the screen than is possible with conventional television viewing, these facilities open up new possibilities for symbolic creativity and begin to blur the line between consumption and production.

Not everyone can afford to buy into the 'video revolution', however. Official figures collected for the *Family Expenditure Survey* show a strong relation between income and access to a VCR. In 1986 for example, only 14.3 per cent of households with a weekly income of £81–100 could afford one. This figure more than doubles to 31.7 per cent among households earning £151–175, and more than doubles again to 64.5 per cent in households with income above £550. Even those owning a VCR can't always afford to use it as much as they might like. In mid-1988 it cost an average of £1.40 to hire a prerecorded tape from a local rental shop. Often it was more, making it a luxury that people had to think twice about. As one young, recently married Wolverhampton woman explains:

> You used to be able to get two for £1.50, and we used to go on a Wednesday. It was cheaper on a Wednesday . . . Then it stopped all of a sudden like and they went up to about £2.00 each. I mean it was a lot then, so we stopped for a bit. We've had a few since . . . At the moment we're trying to save for a holiday, so to pay £2.50, well . . . you could say I could spend that on a holiday like.

The question of equal access becomes more significant when we consider video's potential as a fully fledged production technology allowing TV-literate young people to produce their own images, sounds and re-creations in and of their own informal cultures, and for wider potential 'broadcasting'.

For more than twenty years enthusiasts have been predicting a revolution in which the introduction of cheap, portable, easy-to-operate video cameras would usher in a new era of popular image-making which would allow people to record their lives and experiences and to express their views in their own voice. It hasn't quite happened yet, but there are evident stirrings. The new generation of compact video cameras finally provides the technological means. Whereas it was once a spectacle or a surprise, video cameras are now appearing routinely at weddings, engagement parties, birthdays and informal gatherings. Actualizing this potential for the generality of youth's symbolic work, however, will require an organizational infrastructure capable of providing access to the technology and training in its use and perhaps the developing of new forms of community distribution for the finished products.

Micro-computers

Micros have a variety of uses that relate directly to the organization of pleasure and creativity in the leisure of many young people, though it is a technology which comprehensively seems to exclude women and low-income groups. Of the 33 per cent of UK 16–24-year-olds living in a household possessing a micro in 1987, most were in relatively affluent homes. Only 4.6 per cent of those in households with a weekly income of £81–100 and 9.6 per cent of those in households in the £151–175 income band had access to a machine for example.[2]

Most young people use their machines predominantly for games-playing. From the vantage point of many adult observers, this looks like a relatively trivial pursuit. But to many of those involved it is a richly creative and social activity which provides both an imaginative space and a basis for friendships and sociability.

Games involve a variety of capacities, ranging from hand–eye co-ordination to bargaining, empathy and complex reasoning. In this situation people are no longer viewing a screen. They are interacting with it so that the progress or outcome of the scenario they are faced with depends in large part on their actions. Active symbolic work is not just internal, it has external effects, which in turn react back with obvious potentials for the development of grounded aesthetics.

The more skilled users like Terry, an unemployed 21-year-old in the Leicester study, regularly write their own games:

> Well, games are nice to play but I always have a go, I say 'I wonder if I could make that game' and then I try it myself. Sometimes people come and say 'That's a nice program, did you buy it' and I say, 'No I made it'. My talent seems to lie in making it look better ... For a start, I look for a different presentation; the title screen, etc., adding all little items like that ... One of me greatest achievements was writing me own adventure program where I could slot in any adventure I wanted. Certain problems would always occur, like you having to find a key to get through a door, or using a box to climb on to a shelf, that sort of problem. But also a maze which would calculate whether you could go through a wall with a magical potion or whatever. So you could move around and put little descriptions and everything into it.

It is not necessary to be as committed as Terry, however, to use a micro for creative production. Providing you have the right equipment and programs, home computers offer a range of opportunities for self-expression.

Here, as in other areas then, there is a strong case for positive animation projects and publicly available resource centres, offering not only access to the equipment but also to training and support in its use.

Micro-computer users can also interact with other users or with a central data store, using a telecommunications link. Users can be linked in a vertical configuration with a central computer store of data and information. This has some interesting, but as yet largely unrealized, applications. For example, it could be used to allow young people to consult a community-based data store providing information of particular relevance to them, using a terminal installed in public locations and accessible at a zero or nominal charge.

One way that 'vertical' communications networks are being used already, however, is for 'hacking', that is, making an unauthorized entry into a database without paying the fee, or (in the case of governmental, military and corporate bases) without the necessary security clearance. The most spectacular recent instance is the case of 23-year-old Edward Austin Singh who used terminals at the University of Surrey to break into 250 protected databases around the world. As with all hackers he used a pseudonym. He chose Sredni Vashtar, a ferret in a short story by Saki, but in a moment of high farce the University assumed they were dealing with a Russian spy.

Singh's level of expertise and ingenuity was unusual enough to put him among the hacking élite. But in more modest forms the cracking of protection codes on commercial software or breaking into various other kinds of protected data stores is not an unusual activity among young computer enthusiasts. One young Leicester man used his experience to win a bet with his father.

> It's a program that's very simple to make. It just keeps jiggling combinations. It's a system a lot have used to crack telephone numbers, 'cause this place is ex-directory, and me dad said 'You can't do it in a week' and I said 'Yes, I can'. And using the number plan and the telephone book and a bit of guesswork as well, I located the number. And he says 'I backed you £20 that you can't do it in a week.' And I got my sister involved in it as well, and we ended up taking £40 off him. Served him right.

Usually there is no financial gain involved. The pleasure and grounded aesthetic are in solving the puzzle and beating the system. As another respondent explained,

> I must admit I do have great fun trying to crack protection systems. But that's more to do with the fun of it, rather than anything to do with the program once you've got it on tape.

Computers connected together through the telecommunications system also allow users to communicate with each other without going through a central point. This is the principle behind the increasing number of bulletin boards and message systems, where users create electronic mailboxes and electronic magazines. Again there is huge and yet unrealized potential here for the extension and development of young people's symbolic work and creativity.

Our fundamental point here is that the new screen-based technologies shouldn't be seen as simply extending television services. They have or could have their own specific cultural practices. The new screen-based technologies are not widely available or used at the moment, but their potentials are immense. They need to be understood and developed in a very open and experimental way as providing new spaces for interaction which break down the conventional distinctions between passive viewers and active producers in ways which facilitate the creative symbolic work already in play in the common cultures of young people.

Film

Films provide an important leisure activity for young people. They spend £281 million a year on video purchase and hire and on going to the cinema.[3] Around a third of young people say they see films in the cinema with two-thirds watching at home (22 per cent VCR, 42 per cent TV).[4]

Young people are the age group most represented in cinema audiences. Although working-class young people in the 1940s were the primary viewers, today middle-class young people, and more specifically students, are the primary viewers.[5]

Our fieldwork in Wolverhampton bears out the general finding that young working-class people rarely go to the cinema. For instance, 16-year-old Robert mentions that he goes:

> Not very often. I mean, if there's something good on, I probably will go and see *Crocodile Dundee II*, you know, I'd like to see that. But I don't really go every week, it's just when there's a film on I want to watch. If not, I don't bother.

Still others, who go even less often, suggest that this is because going to the cinema is so costly. Thus Beverly says: 'I haven't found many films that [it's worth] really, most of the time, to pay £1.50 to go and see. The last time I went to the cinema was to see, um, *Rambo*.'

This does not mean necessarily that they prefer to see films in the home. Many of the young people we spoke to have videos but hardly use them. Immediately after purchase frequency of video hirings was very high, but fell off rather sharply after the initial period. This finding reflects other research.[6] Cost may also be a factor in limiting video hire over time. As Susan says, 'Now we've bought the video we can't afford the videos to watch!'

Whatever the cost comparisons and difficulties, it was clear that for many young people cinema provides a 'better' atmosphere than the home. It has its own particular grounded aesthetic. No doubt more working-class young people would attend the cinema more often if they could afford it:

> THERESA: I go for atmosphere.
> BEVERLY: It's better for watching it there.
> THERESA: It's better to watch the picture with a bigger group of people than watching it with a video. 'Cause it's the atmosphere round you, like.
> JC: What about it?
> THERESA: Well, like with *Golden Child*, I was nearly deaf with the laughing, because it's so funny. And in like *Rocky IV*,

everybody, everybody was clapping and saying, 'Come on
Rocky.' And in the end they were clapping and that, and
cheering . . . The Russian was a baddy and everybody booed
when he came on. But when Rocky came on, they were
cheering and that.

The cinema seems to make film viewing a much more social
experience. Theresa's comments suggest that there is a quality of
the pantomime in cinema viewing, with its high level of audience
participation. This is especially true in films like *Rocky IV* which,
like pantomimes, clearly designate 'baddies' and 'goodies'. Young
people take pleasure out of interacting with one another when
watching such films. There is a grounded aesthetic in laughing,
clapping and booing together.

Eighteen-year-old Theresa points out another element of
atmosphere:

THERESA: There's a difference between watching it [a film] on a
little screen and watching it on cinema.
JC: What's the difference?
THERESA: You don't . . . see the whole picture the way it's been
taken.
JC: What do you mean?
THERESA: You don't because the cinema is that wide, it's
rectangular, when the TV screen is square. . . . When you see
a video film, you see it in the television screen, you . . . have a
black bit at the top and bottom, because the cinema screen is
rectangular.

Our subjects brought up issues of sociality and film technical
quality when discussing their favourite films – horror films. These
general issues may take specific forms with different film genres.
Muktar notes that he likes to see horror films at the cinema
because he finds that the size of the screen enhances the horrific
effect: 'It's even more scary in the cinema . . . Because you got the
big object like . . .' Others noted that watching the same film at
home, especially alone, could be even more frightening for different
reasons. While the screen may not be as large, the film may engulf
the viewer in other ways:

MUKTAR: But if you're watching that film at home alone, then
it could scare you, can't it? . . . But if you go to the cinema,
you can't really [be scared]. 'Cause you got that many people
laughing and talking and messing around. They take it as a
joke, you know what I mean?

BEVERLY: Yeah, 'cause some films, like, what is it, *Nightmare on Elm Street*, that could scare you if you're by yourself.

THERESA: I wouldn't watch it by myself. I wouldn't watch any horror film by myself.

JC: You wouldn't . . .

THERESA: I couldn't, I couldn't; I'm just tellin' ya, when I go upstairs to bed at night, when I'm downstairs by myself, I put all the lights on first . . . When I'm downstairs right, and I'm watching the TV, I'm the only one watching the TV, and it's all dark, I put all the lights on.

Horror films seem to work in part through their challenging and tingling invitation to the viewer to take part in the construction of terror. The horror film is enjoyable because of the very familiarity of the path which breeds terror. The horror film presumes that its readers are filmically (horror) literate. It matters that the viewer has seen many horror films before. This is how they know what is coming next, and know that the film presumes that they know what is coming next. This is what brings a sense of immediacy where you can count seconds passing.

Young viewers seem to be very willing participants in this work of mutual symbolic construction, of taking the cues to construct their own grounded aesthetic of horror.

JC: I don't understand what's the fun about horror, about being scared.

THERESA: You enjoy being frightened.

DELROY: What's the point, what is the point of watching a horror film if it's not gonna scare you?

THERESA: Exactly . . . I love being frightened.

JC: What's so good about all this violence?

DELROY: No, but, what's the, what's the point of watching a horror film if it's not gonna scare ya, it's a waste of time.

JC: What's the point of watching a horror film, why do you even want to bother being scared?

DELROY: For the enjoyment of it, because afterwards you go, 'Wow, it was bad!'

The magnification of feelings which the horror film engenders enables the viewer to become fully immersed in the present situation, to experience it intensely. Pleasure comes from conscious symbolic interaction with the film on a scale with many points.

DELROY: It's just that some people are very, how can I put it, believing. The more believing you are, the more scared you are.

Others can be more resistant and pride themselves on it even though it might take a little help from their friends:

> BEVERLY: I like the challenge . . . Yeah, 'cause you watch these things to see if you're gonna get scared.
> THERESA: Yeah, if you watch it, you're brave. If you watch all of it.
> MUKTAR: You have to watch all of it with your mates, then you're not gonna chicken out, are you?

The horror genre seems almost to conspire to make its construction of reality overlap with that of the viewer. It does so partly by its supposition that the viewer is familiar with the genre, with blood, gore and terror. But it also does this by having ordinary young people as protagonists and figures for identification. The sense of the overlap of the horrific and the real is enhanced when films are supposedly based on real stories, and by constructing filmic images as being really capable of changing the behaviour of the viewer in horrendous ways.

> THERESA: I think the best is *Amityville Horror*. That's supposed to be a true story.
> DELROY: And another one that's true, eh, it's old now, is called *Texas Chain Saw Massacre* . . . It's a true story.
> THERESA: That's why I don't think little children should get into horror films because, I mean, they're easy to copy, the little children copy things like that.
> DELROY: Yeah, it's true, because . . . this girl's mum right, the girl's about eight, nine . . . and she thought that her mum was ignoring her, and she watched this film, she was watching the television, and she saw this baby drop a doll on its head. So she went up to the baby and did the same thing, and killed it.

Ironically, 'copycat' theories may have their main practical effect in symbolically heightening the experience of filmic horror rather than in illuminating how such horror might influence real behaviour outside the filmic experience. It is the intermingling of horror and reality and the viewers' role in producing both that produce the shiver and tingle.

In fact there are several countervailing strategies developed and used by young viewers themselves to push back the shady boundaries distinguishing horror from reality.

This is also an area of creative symbolic work, of developed 'reading' pleasures in the construction of specific grounded aesthetics. One strategy is to focus on deciphering the special effects with which the feeling of terror is constructed. As Delroy notes, people like to see things with good effects, with lots of effects. These produce terrifyingly pleasurable experience because they engender simultaneously fear and appreciation of artifice.

Viewers derive pleasure from watching and trying to understand how images appear real but are not. The process of fabrication is celebrated: the viewer simultaneously appreciates and dissects. This is the ability, undoubtedly built up through years of watching television, to read and experience images at the same time. This may be helped by seeing the film in the 'proper' context: 'When you're with friends, right, you can laugh and joke afterwards.' By laughing with friends at the terrifying bits, one can put the feelings of terror in perspective, acknowledge artifice and affirm one's own sense of reality. Joking, re-enacting bits of or spoofing the film afterwards elaborate the specific grounded aesthetics through which the film was made to come alive and establish and reinforce the group as a social symbolic unit, reminding everyone that the horror effect is just an artificial accomplishment.

The young, then, do not simply assess horror films using the terms and strategies that the genre provides. They also use other interpretive skills which they have acquired from their filmic and televisual viewing more generally. They also evaluate a film partly by putting themselves in the place of the protagonist. If the actions of the protagonist fit with their understanding of how such a person would act, then they find the film compelling. They use their general social experience. Theresa on Freddy Krueger in *Elm Street Part I*:

> THERESA: I think he wanted the strongest person the last so he could have a good battle with them, the strongest – strong-minded person. So he got rid of the weakest first. If I was Freddy Krueger, I would do that . . .

Finally, at least some young people evaluate films using quasi-political criteria. Theresa, for example, mentions that perhaps the best thing about the *Nightmare on Elm Street* films is their portrayal of women.

> THERESA: The heroine, I mean. I'm glad it was a girl, though, this time.
> JC: Okay, let's hear it, why?
> THERESA: I think the best part was when the girl was doin' somersaults. I mean, that was, that was just brilliant. 'Cause I mean, I mean . . . at least men don't think, can't look down on us and think we're stupid and that.

JC: Yeah?
BEVERLY: 'Cause that's how films, that's how films portray
women, that they're stupid, they're only there for one thing,
and when they're running away, they'll run off and trip over
and hurt their ankle . . . And at the end, right, they just, they
end up just kissing and falling in love with the hero. Whereas
this one, right, there was a heroine and, uh, you know, she
was strong, she had a strong personality.

Of course, Theresa could not make an observation like this if there
were not a self-conscious move on the part of the film-makers to
present an alternative view of women. But Theresa not only picks
on this alternative representation, she hails it as centrally important. In this and other ways film-watching is an interactive and
active process involving its own kind of symbolic work and
creativity. Those concerned to develop culture and cultural policy
may need to watch audiences, not films.

'What's your favourite ad?'

Young people's creative responses to advertisements are shaped by
the way advertisers themselves fashion their products. Crucial here
is a recent move by advertisers, it seems, to design their products to
give aesthetic pleasure to be enjoyed in and for itself. Research and
survey results on customer preference and life style are not now the
only resources which advertisers turn to. They also turn to *artistic*
resources, to art-school graduates and established film-makers.

The fusion of advertising with other expressive forms is also
evident in the borrowing of actors from film and television to play
characters in advertisements. Not only do such actors draw on
theatrical skills and conventions which are then subsumed into the
commercial form, they also carry with them their theatrical identities which then work to enhance selective meanings. Furthermore, advertising images and narratives increasingly rely on and
parody those that come from other expressive forms like film and
pop videos. Advertisers rework and elaborate these images and
narratives to fit their own purposes. They also make advertisements that sometimes quote their own, or others', prior advertisements. In making these advertisements they presume that the
viewer is televisually literate.

These more complex and sophisticated products are often aimed
especially at young people. Advertisers assume – and in part produce – young people as very much more tele-literate than people of

other ages. Indeed, no other age group is considered as discriminating, cynical and resistant to the 'hard sell'. Furthermore, no other group is as astute at decoding the complex messages, cross references and visual jokes of current advertising.

Young people see other media forms with great frequency. They have grown up on new and more sophisticated media forms. These forms increasingly invite the viewer to 'read' them, providing the viewer with the necessary symbolic tools. Consequently, young people have developed very complex interpretive and creative capacities. They have the capacity to consume commercials independently of the product which is being marketed. Commercials can be cultural products in themselves and consumed for themselves. Thus the success of any particular commercial is, in this respect, separate from its effectiveness in promoting sales. More precisely, perhaps, the effectiveness of an advertisement in producing brand name familiarity at least, now often works through its autonomous quality as a symbolic communication.

These developments in the advertising industry clearly affect how young people see advertisements and the possibilities for a creative symbolic relationship with them. It's now a topic of conversation, 'What's your favourite ad?' This would have been a laughable question not so long ago. The new shape that advertisers have given to advertisements, and their explicit focus on young people have enabled adverts to become tokens in young people's system of social exchange. Here is an extract from one of our group discussions on the media:

THERESA: What's your favourite advertisement?

JC: I'm trying to think.

THERESA: Have you see the one with the raisins? . . . It's brilliant!

JC: What's this? [T and several others sing 'Heard it on the Grapevine'].

THERESA: That's brilliant. And I like the Vita Lite [margarine] one [sings advert to tune of old song 'Israelites', accompanied by Beverly].

JC: When you watch the telly, do you watch adverts too?

TERESA, BEVERLY AND SHARMA: Yeah.

BEVERLY: Because they're good. Some are better than the programmes, man.

THERESA: I mean, some of them have even got into the charts . . . My favourite one is Vita Lite and the raisins. They are brilliant. Ace! Because the first time I saw it [the raisin advert], I thought the couple was real. And what it was, it was

made out of plasticine, like. And I thought it was brilliant. I
liked how the raisins come out and they just . . .
BEVERLY: They dance.
THERESA: They just burned off, they just burned off, you know
. . . And I like Vita Lite. I like the song. 'Cause I got the
original song.
JC: What is it?
BEVERLY: [sings] 'Wake up in the morning when the sun is
breaking'.
BEVERLY, THERESA AND SHARMA: [sing] 'Oh, oh, oh, Vita Lite!'
[all laugh].

Whilst many older people find advertisements an irritation,
Theresa and her friends consider them to be expressive forms
capable of giving symbolic pleasure, whose ability to produce
pleasure can be evaluated. There is now a generation gap in reading
advertisements.

The mere mention of perhaps the most memorable of these
advertisements makes them begin to sing the accompanying tunes.
They take pleasure in singing these songs in unison. They provide
evidence of the similarity of assumedly internally constituted
taste, of shared grounded aesthetics.

Old pop songs are given new meanings by being connected with
images in advertisements:

THERESA: You just listen carefully to the song so you can
understand what the advert. is trying to tell you. And when
you see the pictures, you um try and work out what the
song's got to do with that.

There are analogies here with the quoting of old songs in house
music. In both cases, the old song is recycled in a new context,
enabling new meanings to be spun out. The raisins advertisement,
for example, makes a pun of the meaning of the expression 'through
the grapevine'. Young people recognize, as Theresa does, that
advertisements juxtapose images and tunes but do not completely
conjoin them. Advertisements invite the viewer to do so, using the
materials that they provide.

Young people enjoy the active role they are asked to play and
which they can creatively elaborate and go beyond. This is a
possibility usually absent in those many TV shows which they say
are 'worse than the advertisements'.

Young people do not just enjoy putting together and then reading
disparate symbolic elements. They also enjoy developing a
familiarity with the images and songs that are presented. Theresa
again:

You like to hear something which you can remember. And it does stick. Most of the adverts you hear do stick, certain phrases. Even when it's really stupid, you just remember what they say. And you can take the piss out of it or you can do what you like.

Advertisements quote not only other genres but also themselves. This requires familiarity with the originals. But Theresa and her friends do not simply perform the symbolic feats that advertisements invite them to. They also criticize the way in which advertisements structure these feats. They evaluate their efficacy in their own terms. Collectively criticizing advertisements affirms the evaluative criteria that young people themselves are developing. Young people, for instance, assess special effects and their ability to produce images. They take pleasure in the lengths to which advertisers go to fabricate an image and scrutinize their own reactions to analyse how the reality effect has been materially created.

Young people also actively appreciate advertisements that use well-known actors. Recently Lenny Henry featured in an advertisement for Alpen breakfast cereal, in which he acts as several black characters who all like Alpen. This advertisement is described by Delroy, Theresa and Beverly:

DELROY: I know the one that I like, that Lenny 'enry one.

THERESA: Yes! Alpen . . . 'One Alpen, then there's two Alpen!'

BEVERLY: 'Winston!' [all laugh] 'Ya want some more?'

JC: Wait, I haven't seen it. Could you explain it?

DELROY: It's, um, Lenny 'enry's, um, playing the characters of about four people, right. The mum, the Rasta, . . .

BEVERLY: . . . the grandfather, . . .

DELROY: . . . and the son.

JC: And what's so good about it?

DELROY: It's just the way he does it. It's like imitating black people and it's just good.

THERESA: I like the way he imitates black people, the way they talk.

DELROY: He goes, 'It's not just something, it's crucial' [in unison with Theresa and Beverly].

THERESA: It's like, it has each character talk about the actual cereal. Like, you know, the mister supercool talking, like, 'Hey' [said in cool tone].

BEVERLY: 'Anyone for seconds?' [laughs].

THERESA: The grandad talks, you know, the old Jamaican . . . And, um, the young boy talks about the younger generation.

This group takes symbolic pleasure from the advertisement because they know that enjoying it requires a grounded aesthetic
response to Henry's skills as an actor as well as knowledge of
Henry's roles. They act out the scripts and jokes with relish and
with their own kind of emphasis and energy.

Do these new self-conscious advertisements make young people
buy things – manipulate them in the end, no matter through what
open appearances of symbolic participation? The discussion about
the raisin advertisement took a surprising twist which is relevant
here:

> JC: So when you see these adverts, do they have anything to do
> with you buying the product?
> DELROY: I don't think so.
> BEVERLY: I don't buy them.
> THERESA: I'm gonna buy the raisin . . . They've got the figurine
> of it, like a teddy bear. £5.99. And I'm gonna get one. 'Cause I
> think it's brilliant! He's [the shop owner] got the one with
> the glove and the one with the sunglasses as well.
> JC: But you wouldn't buy raisins?
> THERESA: I don't like raisins.

The products which advertisements induce us to buy may be
composed just of images, artificially created images sometimes
made for the unsuccessful promotion of other more substantial
commodities! Undoubtedly we'll see the promotion of images grow
– the ever more selective promotion of promotion. This is clearly
manipulative to an extent, but the active ways in which 'the
consumer' has been brought into the process and the scope for
individual choice and creativity for meaning and identity construction should not be underestimated. This, at the very least, is not
'mass marketing' and can't be shot down with the same 'anti-mass'
blunderbuss arguments. Theresa's 'consumption' is one which
signals her individuality. Not everyone is interested. None of the
others in this group wanted a raisin figurine. It has resonances only
for Theresa and symbolizes quite effectively, therefore, part of her
identity. The process of buying and consumption can itself be
symbolically creative in the line of a specific grounded aesthetic.

Young people do not have a free choice from a wide range of
symbolic materials, through which to exercise their symbolic
work. The range is constricted and supplied for reasons other than
their own cultural development. But young people certainly respond creatively to open and usable resources when, for whatever
reason, they are available. Recognizing this, not sniffing at the

materials or condemning why they are provided, is what should engage our sense of possibility.

Magazines

Although some of the music papers date from before World War II, a magazine market for young people is a post-war phenomenon, developing in tandem with the expansion of particular commodity markets, records, fashion, make-up and toiletries, targeted at the newly discovered affluent youth market. Until the early 1980s this magazine market was dominated by IPC (International Publishing Corporation) and D. C. Thomson of Dundee, although the National Magazine Company (in the shape of *Cosmopolitan* and *Company*) had made some inroads during the 1970s. Available categories of magazine included the music papers (male), photo-story and fashion/feature magazines (female). But in the first half of the 1980s, with the launch of several new magazines, the profile and ownership of the market was reshaped. By 1989 EMAP, a publisher based in Peterborough and until the 1980s better known for bike and photography magazines, had become the most successful 'youth' publisher. Its clutch of titles includes *Smash Hits* and *Just Seventeen*, 'copied' by IPC in the shape of *No 1* and *Mizz* respectively. Together with the independently owned *Face* magazine (plus its competitors *i-D* and *Blitz*) EMAP challenged the assumptions about what was appropriate for a young readership and how such magazines should be produced.

Changes included:

- Technological developments facilitating shorter lead times so that magazines could be more 'newsy', delivering higher-quality printing at the same price, allowing magazines to stand up to radio, TV and pop promotions.
- Editorial teams who, if they weren't quite producing magazines for themselves, were in touch with the age group they were addressing, and banished the patronizingly paternal address of older magazines such as *Jackie*.
- Introduction of design styles which acknowledge readers as, on the one hand, skilful at interpreting images and text and, on the other, as 'wandering', 'cruising' or 'drifting' across a magazine rather than reading it, word by word, image by image, so that parts of magazines link up with a variety of other media, and with other concerns, beyond the page, assuming the knowledgeable reader as active agent in making creative links.

Jackie's circulation and several of IPC's titles are slowly falling whilst those of the newer magazines are buoyant or rising. Eighteen per cent of 15–24-year-olds read *Jackie* and 4 per cent *Mizz*. Three per cent read *The Face*. At the sharp 'style' end of the magazine market, at least, readership figures suggest that gender differences are diminishing; compare the 73-per-cent male to 27-per-cent female readership of *NME* to *The Face*'s 62-per-cent male, 38-per-cent female, and *Blitz*'s 42-per-cent male, 58-per-cent female readership.[7]

Unlike newspapers, magazines are regarded by young people as 'interesting': 'All of it is relevant to me; it contains things I enjoy.' The magazine form – 'light reading, varied topics', 'different articles suit different moods' – is seen as important because the reader 'can flip from beginning to end and over and over'. This might seem like young people's opting for the easy read, for anything that isn't too much work. But there is another form of symbolic work involved: the need to actually exercise the invited control over what and how much is read and with what degree of attention and with what links to outside events and experiences. In contrast, with a book the reader is usually hijacked by the narrative.

Magazines also directly address young people; 'the articles are on a more one to one level (compared to newspapers)'. These aspects, combined with the fact that the young person has probably bought the magazine her/himself, renders the magazine as 'hers/his', a possession symbolically important in the creation of a self-identity, as such magazines are carefully kept after reading, even if never returned to again.

Young women and increasingly young men develop their external image in part by using magazine hints on fashion and appearance.

> ANGELA: *Mizz*, that's a good book for fashion. *Smash Hits* and things like that. You just see clothes and you think, I like that . . .
>
> JO: I get *Vogue, Just Seventeen* . . . Well, it's my sister who gets it, so I have a look at it, you know, and *Over 21* for all the fashion . . .
>
> JC: Tell me about *Mizz*.
>
> ANGELA: Well, it has people wearing clothes that haven't come in, like, you know, and then you start seeing people wearing them.

These young women, and others, report that they also get their fashion ideas from looking carefully at people on the streets, at how their friends dress and at television shows like *The Clothes Show*.

Keeping up with the ever changing world of fashion is difficult for these young women, given their limited resources. Doing so and developing a stylistic grounded aesthetic is of utmost importance to them. Figuring out how to dress their bodies requires that they learn a subtle symbolic system, and then decide which of its components fit with, express and develop in desirable ways their identity. But, establishing their identity, they also walk the tightrope between an individual sense of themselves, and a construction which obeys the rules of what a woman is *meant* to look like. Many young women respond to fashion images whilst at the same time being critical of magazine imagery: 'They pressurize you to be attractive/beautiful, etc. like models'; 'I become increasingly depressed seeing sylphlike women when I'm on the plump side!'

For young black people *Ebony* is a popular magazine which provides ideas about how to dress in ways which enable them to express a black identity tangibly, materially, on the surface of their bodies. According to Theresa *Ebony* also offers a wider positive self-image. It tells her:

> THERESA: About black people in America, and how they reached fame and fortune and successful careers, and hair products and clothes . . .
>
> JC: So what kinds of things do you learn by reading about the successful American blacks?
>
> THERESA: Well, personally, I think it makes you think anybody can reach anywhere as long as you put your mind to it, just a bit of motivation.

The magazine emphasizes inner qualities alone as providing enough tools to change the circumstances of black people, disregarding the external, social constraints that are often placed in their way. Whether Theresa actually believes this or enjoys the bolstering of self which the myth provides is debatable. An article is not read for one meaning, but can be variously interpreted, not just between readers, but by the same reader over time or even simultaneously as parts of the differing tasks of their symbolic work, according to different specific grounded aesthetics.

The advice columns in magazines tend to be much read and provide young women with symbolic materials concerning their personal and family lives. They can also be much criticized and parodied in their symbolic work and creativity:

> HILARY: The problem pages! 'Dear Aunt Clara, I fancy this boy in my class and he do fancy me. I've asked him out and he's told me to fuck off. Please will you help me.'

JC: What's the advice?
HILARY: Find someone else, love, don't worry about him.
YVONNE: They just say, let this boy make his move when he
    wants and make yourself look nice for him, and he'll make
    his move if he really fancies you. If not, forget him.

These young women are at one and the same time recognizing the
'genre' of problem pages, sending them up and, in Yvonne's case,
dismissing the traditional view of relationships in which girls are
simply passive bystanders. Yvonne's capacity to question this
assumption suggests that she is working on and through the symbolic system offered by problem pages to a more expansive and
empowering one.

Young women can also be highly critical of 'soppy' love stories,
whilst at the same time enjoying them in moving beyond
them.

HILARY: These are the kind of stories that the magazines have:
    Sarah was 16, and her packed Andy in for Steve, but she
    found out that Steve loved her more than whatever his name
    was and he was knocking off someone else. What could she
    do, she used to cry at night. At the end they get back together
    and that's the end of the story. And that's all that ever
    happens.

The fact that Hilary dismisses the happy ending suggests that she
uses the symbols with which romantic love is constructed in a
different way to that proposed, one which takes into account a more
complex and realistic understanding of relationships.

Young people also use symbolic resources from magazines to
resonate leisure interests along the line of particular grounded
aesthetics. Bill, for instance, decorates his room with Wolves'
football team memorabilia: pictures from magazines, articles of
clothing and bits of information about his favourite team. Such
young men are expressing, at the most intimate level, not just their
support for their local team, but the place that support has in the
construction of their identities.

Young women, and some young men, use articles about pop stars
as a resource they can work on further, as Katy, Rachel, Jo and
Angela explain:

JC: Is there stuff about music or stars?
RACHEL: Stars, fact files. Like one person out of a group, and it
    gives you your [sic] name, birthdate, interest, hobbies, mar-
    ried, dislikes, favourite food, music, cars . . . Like it tells you
    how they made their video.

JO: They write the song out and it's there for you. So when it's on you can sing along [laughs] in your bedroom. I learn all the words from it.

JC: Do you ever cut things out of magazines and put them on the walls? What kind of things do you cut out?

JO: Posters. Pop stars.

JC: Do you ever make posters with little things from them?

KATY: I done this facts cover about George Michael, 'cause I'm crazy on him. I got all the fact files and music, song words and all that.

JC: Do you put that on them all or cut it out?

KATY: I just like made a book into it, like. Scrapbook . . .

Young women use their preferences for one star over another to help delineate the criteria they consider important in relationships and to see how they differ from their peers in their 'taste' in men. Pop stars are, to some extent, symbolic vehicles with which young women understand themselves more fully, even if, by doing so, they partly shape their personalities to fit the stars' alleged preferences. At the same time, in developing a relationship with the male pin-up decorating her bedroom wall, she is doing what the male does – imagining, in a controlled way, how to place this man in her life.

These activities often occur in 'bedroom culture',[8] the most private space in which young women act and interact with each other and develop affective grounded aesthetics. The bedroom is a place where young women talk among themselves and try to understand their relationships with parents, siblings and boyfriends. More significantly, in doing so, they are learning to articulate the emotional criteria with which the inner self is constituted. They learn, that is, about their own and other people's motives by closely scrutinizing all the relationships in which they are involved.

The symbolic resources on offer in magazines are involved in both the creation of specific grounded aesthetics and in the establishment of many young women's self-identities. And yet heavy reliance on magazines as a source of creativity in 'bedroom cultures' and their place in the construction of a feminine identity are also the result of expectations and constraints which make it difficult for young women to engage in less introverted cultural activities. If magazines culturally *em*power young women, they are also products of their power*less*ness. Magazines are a safe pleasure and resource but we should look for ways of providing conditions which might enable women to risk more in their creativity.

Notes

1 *Cultural Trends*, Issue I, Policy Studies Institute, 1989.
2 *Family Expenditure Survey*, HMSO, 1987.
3 CJMR *Annual Media Income and Spending Survey*, 1987.
4 Reported in D. Docherty, D. Morrison and M. Tracey, *The Last Picture Show*, British Film Institute, 1987.
5 Docherty *et al.*, op. cit.
6 Docherty *et al.*, op. cit.
7 *National Readership Survey*, July 1987 – June 1988, Joint Industry for National Readership Surveys (JICNARS).
8 See McRobbie, A. and Garber, J. (1975) 'Girls and subcultures: an exploration' in S. Hall and T. Jefferson (eds), *Resistance Through Rituals: Youth Cultures in Post-war Britain*, Hutchinson, 1975.

—3—
Music and symbolic creativity

Popular music is a tremendously important site of common culture, for individual and collective symbolic work and creativity. The message of all youth research in the last thirty years has been that popular music is young people's central cultural interest. This blanket finding conceals many variations in what such interest means, for behind the category of 'youth' lies an enormous diversity of taste groups, subcultures and audiences, differentiated by class, race and gender.

What is clear, however, is that young people's musical activities, whatever their cultural background or social position, rest on a substantial and sophisticated body of knowledge about popular music. Most young people have a clear understanding of its different genres, and an ability to hear and place sounds in terms of their histories, influences and sources. Young musicians and audiences alike have no hesitation about making and justifying judgements of meaning and value.

Despite this, most official thinking and writing on popular music, particularly within the arts, is still informed by common sense notions of it as trivial and banal, as a simple-minded and uncultured activity that is commercially parasitic and artistically worthless. Beneath such notions are a number of deep-rooted assumptions about the arts which regard musical performance as creative, and consumption as passive. In most arts writing, this distinction between production and consumption, amateur and professional, is taken for granted as a matter of individual skill, talent and creativity.

Within popular music, and within young people's own musical practices, however, such distinctions are a good deal less clear cut. Symbolic creativity bridges them. The special relationship between production and consumption in popular music culture means that most pop musicians begin as fans and create by copying sounds from records and cassettes: they become producers as consumers. Most musical activity, then, begins as and from consumption, from the process of listening to music. But consumption itself is creative. The cultural meaning of Bros or Morissey, house or hip-hop, Tiffany or Tracey Chapman, isn't simply the result of record-company sales campaigns, it depends too on consumer abilities to make value judgements, to talk knowledgeably and passionately about their genre tastes, to place music in their lives, to use commodities and symbols for their own imaginative purposes and to generate their own particular grounded aesthetics. These processes involve the exercise of critical, discriminating choices and uses which disrupt the taste categories and 'ideal' modes of consumption promoted by the leisure industry and break up its superimposed definitions of musical meaning.

To describe pop as passive is to ignore these vital cultural processes. For it is as important to understand how consumers' discriminating abilities are learnt and sustained as it is to discover why, in some circumstances, young pop fans become committed to performing for themselves. This chapter looks at young people's lived experience of music and their symbolic work in and on it. It looks at some of the common creative practices that young people engage in around popular music, at the grounded aesthetics from which music-making sometimes proceeds.

The chapter draws from interviews and discussions with a group of some twenty young people aged 18 to 26 in the Birmingham area, from the Wolverhampton ethnography, from prior ethnographic research into young people's use of music[1] and from selective examples drawn from music journals, and other Birmingham based informal publications. Where not otherwise indicated quotes in this chapter come from the Birmingham group.

The creative consumption of musical forms

Listening and buying

Many of the young people we interviewed frequently listen to the radio, particularly local radio and Radio 1 (still a staple of young people's listening). The purposes and uses of radio listening were multiple: to hear and tape new music, to listen to a specific show or an individual disc jockey (DJ), to use the radio for company during the night or day, or to structure and punctuate the daily routine of getting up, getting ready for work/college, working and relaxing.

Some young people use radio in the time-honoured way as an accompaniment to specific activities, such as domestic work in the home, using different programmes for different kinds of activities. In addition to local, commercial and national radio, pirate radio stations are also highly popular amongst young people, particularly young Afro-Caribbeans, but amongst large numbers of Asian and white youth as well. By catering directly for the musical tastes and enthusiasms of their listeners, pirate radio stations have provided a crucial broadcasting outlet for black music and an important space in which it can be transmitted and heard by young people. The massive popular support that now exists for some local pirate radio stations is indicative of the failure of local, commercial and BBC radio to meet the needs of large sections of young listeners.

For many young people the purchasing of records and tapes is an important sphere of cultural activity in itself, one that can range in intensity from casual browsing to earnest searching for particular records. It is a process that involves clear symbolic work: complex and careful exercises of choice from the point of initial listening to seeking out, handling and scrutinizing records.

With the prohibitive price of new records, and software such as compact discs (CDs), secondhand records have acquired an even greater importance for some young people. Some will spend hours browsing in secondhand record stores, looking for bargains and especially for oldies and revives. Indeed one of the prominent features of young people's current musical activities is their interest in old music, such as 1950s rock'n'roll, 1960s dance music, 1970s soul.

This interest in old music is partly a result of record-company strategies to make more revenue out of growing back catalogues, through rereleases, licensing songs for use in advertising, and releasing oldies and greatest hits compilations. But it also signals an enthusiastic interest in popular music from the 1950s, 1960s and 1970s amongst a generation who never heard such music the first time round, and for whom it is in many senses new – and, for some, more authentic than current styles. The result is that large numbers of young people now do their own archaeologies of popular music history, carefully excavating the originals and tracing the genealogies of particular styles, whether from films, TV clips, magazines, or rereleased. In certain club-based dance cultures amongst the young, musical styles, such as those of 1970s soul and disco, have been excavated and reappropriated as dance music. Amongst some this extends into an avid collecting of old music, scouring secondhand shops for records that can be sold, swapped for others, used for the purposes of 'mixing' live in clubs or for compiling personal tapes. There is a high exchange rate of records, both new and secondhand, between young people, with albums and singles being swapped and borrowed regularly. These are sure signs that the interest in 'vinyl', where it can be acquired cheaply, is still alive amongst some young people.

Home taping

The impoverishing effects of unemployment together with the declining economic importance of the traditional youth music market have resulted in something of a shift in consumption habits amongst the young. One of the most visible examples of that shift has been the massive growth in home taping. This is an important material dimension of symbolic work and creativity.

Home-taping of music is, in one sense, a strategy directly tailored to recession conditions. The tape cassette has proved to be a practical, flexible and cheap way of consuming and distributing music. With many young people unable to afford full-priced, new records, let alone CDs, on a regular basis, cassette tapes have become one of the principal currencies of consumption. Records are increasingly borrowed to be taped, with some young people collecting large stores of tapes, tapes not only of records, but also of live dances, gigs, parties and other musical events.

Taping music from the radio is now a widespread practice amongst the young. Young listeners select their favourite records from the weekly chart run-down and compile their own personal 'pick of the pops'. Alternatively, they tape new, unavailable, or expensive import records (particularly off pirate radio). By skilful manipulation of the pause button on a cassette recorder, and by means of deft cueing and rewinding, they can instantly edit out the spoken interruptions of the DJ, or jingles and commercials:

> JOHN: If I haven't got a record I'll tape it off the radio and, before the DJ starts talking, fade it down. Or new records that friends have got, I'll just tape.

With cheap, twin-deck cassette recorders now widely available, it is also possible to make duplicate copies of tapes themselves, and distribute them informally amongst friends for private consumption or, alternatively, to sell them.

For those who can't afford to buy records, or who don't want to bother with the problems of consumption and choice, home taping is an appropriate solution. This is especially so for young people who own a portable cassette player/radio, but don't have the facilities to record records. Young people frequently rely on friends, with larger record collections to make tapes for them. There is something of an informal hierarchy of taste operating here, with the more committed and avid record collectors used as trusted and accepted consumer guides by some young people. Others request a particular form or style of music (slow-sentimental, uptempo-dance, roots-political) and let the tape compiler select the specific records. This process was amply demonstrated by Mary in Wolverhampton.

> If I want a tape done now, all I do is buy my tape and give it to someone else to tape it for me . . . and I say 'Will you do this for me', and they say 'What do you want', and you tell them what sort of record you want. If they've got it, they'll do it, or if they've got something else different you say, 'OK fair enough, do it for me' . . . They'll do it for you as long as you've got the tape, but if you haven't got the tape you say 'OK, here's the money, you get a tape and you do it for me, whatever change is left you can keep it.'

In this way, cassette tapes enable people to make their own personal soundtracks and compilations. Some young people extend this practice to experimenting with their own mastermixes of dance records according to their own grounded aesthetic – the aim being to mix several records together on a tape in a continuous flow, keeping, for instance the same beat, or to create interesting juxtapositions of different songs, rhythms and melodies.

In these more worked up practices, the tape and the turntable begin to assume the status of instruments in their own right. The hi-fi consumption hardware of the 1980s, such as portable cassette players, have also made the use of taped music (in public spaces especially) more flexible. The portable stereo cassette, in particular, has become something of a popular hi-fi for all. Relatively cheap and widely available through numerous retail outlets, it is truly the Dansette of the 1980s.

Given that cassette tapes occupy such a central position in the consumption and listening habits of young people, it is perhaps not surprising that some should be so resistant to the idea of bringing in a levy on blank tapes, or so contemptuous of arguments that 'home taping is killing music'. To many the economic and cultural logic of taping was plain and simple, and its illegality largely irrelevant. One young man felt that the idea of bringing in a levy to stop home taping was pathetic:

They'll never stop it whatever they do. They put the price of records up, well they're a waste of money as they are. People are still going to buy tapes 'cause they're cheaper. If you can tape a record, why buy it?

(Ignition/Young at Art, p. 16)

Interpreting sounds

Much of the existing research on popular music suggests that songs have their primary impact and appeal as vocal and instrumental sounds, rather than as explicitly verbal or lyrical statements.

This is not to suggest simply that the music is more important than the lyrics in young people's listening, or to place form over content. Rather, it is to suggest that songs bear meaning and allow symbolic work not just as speech acts, but also as structures of sound with unique rhythms, textures and forms. Thus, it is not always what is sung, but the *way* it is sung, within particular conventions or musical genres which gives a piece of music its communicative power and meaning. The sound of a voice and all the extra-linguistic devices used by singers, such as vocal inflections, nuances, hesitations, emphases or sighs, are just as important in conveying meaning as explicit statements, messages and stories.

Our discussions with young people suggest that the rhythms and sounds of popular music do indeed have a capacity to hold particular kinds of meaning and pleasure, and to evoke certain emotions within their listeners. Much popular music produces feelings and affective states, first and foremost, before it produces any specific attitudes or forms of social consciousness; feelings of happiness/ sadness, romance, sexual feelings, or uplifting feelings. In this sense, the power of a particular song lies in its capacity to capture a particular mood or sentiment by a complex combination of different sounds and signifying elements. As one young man said, songs could, in this way, express intimate personal feelings and voice desires: 'Sometimes when I want to express something I can say to a person "Listen to this record – that's the way I'm feeling."' In this way songs can provide symbolic materials towards the formation and articulation of specific grounded aesthetics which are about and enable survival: contesting or expressing feelings of boredom, fear, powerlessness and frustration. They can be used as affective strategies to cope with, manage and make bearable the experiences of everyday life. Perhaps the most heightened example of this is the use of the personal stereo or Walkman, the ultimate artefact in providing a personal soundscape that can be carried around, quite literally, inside the head, while travelling, walking, waiting or negotiating public spaces. One young informant, who at one stage was never to be seen without a Walkman, said that music was absolutely vital to surviving and getting through the day: 'You see this tape and earphones round my neck . . . you know . . . *Must* have music, man! . . . I'd die without music!'

Time and time again, young people pointed out that it was 'the beat' and the rhythm that they liked when accounting for their own musical tastes. These features were felt to be most prominent in black and black-influenced dance music, universally popular amongst black and white youth, male and female. House music was mentioned as being the most popular style of the moment (an uptempo and highly syncopated dance music with lots of over-dubbed cross-rhythms, sampled voices and effects). One informant felt that in house music, as in much other dance music, the words weren't of any real significance. It was the 'feel' behind the music which was more important. For many young people, the syncopations and textures of dance music, through its complex polyrhythms and drum and bass patterns, has the ability to produce a grounded aesthetic of sensual pleasure and to literally move the body, both physically and emotionally. One young woman described reggae and soul as 'heart music':

> JUNE: It's heart music . . . music of the heart, it just gets you right there [lays her hand on her chest] . . . Reggae's like a heartbeat, it's the same kind of rhythm, there's something very crucial about rhythm . . . I'm not sure what it is.

In reggae, specifically, the physical power and prominence of the bass often held the greatest attraction. For some, it explained the overwhelming sensuality of reggae music. As Pete, another young reggae fan, put it: 'It gets you in the gut like . . . Most times I don't listen to the singing. The singing's going on and that, but I listen to the bass.' The effect of the bass and the rhythm, especially in the live context of consumption, often pre-empted the significance of any verbal meanings. These musical features are brought to life, experienced most intensely, and become part of a bodily grounded aesthetic on the dance floor. At parties, discos, dances and live concerts, whether pumped out of speakers through the hardware of a sound system, or transmitted to the crowd from a live band on stage, the music seems to be materialized at the site of the body, to be literally felt as much as heard.

Dance

Dancing is the principal way in which musical pleasures become realized in physical movement and bodily grounded aesthetics. The sensual appeal of popular music is at its greatest in dance music, where its direct courting of sexuality generates a heightened sense of self and body. Experimentation with dance styles involves its own characteristic forms of cultural work and informal, learning processes. Patrick regularly practises and rehearses routines at home, dancing to records with his brother:

> You just stick a record on, and get into the groove kind of thing, like we'll work out some new moves over the weekend, and go up to the Powerhouse on a Monday and try them out like, you know . . . and sometimes you'll get a whole line of people doing it . . . It's really good.

Amongst white youth, many dance styles are initially appropriated and popularized from black youth culture. Imported from America, in the case of soul, funk and hip-hop, or Jamaica, in the case of reggae, they are taken up by young blacks and rapidly transmitted to young whites, who incorporate them into their own repertoires of cultural expression. John, for example, describes how he had picked up a reggae dance style known as 'skanking' (popular in the late 1970s) after seeing it practised by young blacks at a local youth club in South Birmingham:

> That fascinated me, and ever since then I've loved skanking. I picked up on it real fast and I'd practise the moves at home while I'm listening to my records, right. And we'd sort of mess around, me, my sister and my cousin . . . And they'd show me the dances they were learning.

Dance music enjoys mass popularity amongst young people, black and white, male and female alike. Out of the vast numbers of young people who participate in dancing regularly, whether in clubs, pub discos or house parties, there is a sizeable group of 'serious' dancers who concentrate on and even formalize a bodily grounded aesthetic of their own. For this group, the quality of a particular venue and its sound system, the individual DJ, and particularly the music policy, are extremely important. The emphasis is strictly on dancing, sometimes to the exclusion of drinking, or even courting. Young people, particularly the unemployed, will often go to a club with the price of admission, their nightbus fare home and perhaps enough money for one drink.

'All-dayers' are often a focal point for serious dancing and are something of a speciality in the North and the Midlands. Held in particular night clubs, often on a Sunday, they regularly draw crowds of around two thousand people who converge on the venue from as far afield as London and the South-east. These are dance marathons which run for a mammoth nine or ten hours, and where a host of different DJs play a mixed diet of funk, soul, house music, hip-hop, Latin music and jazz.

There are also specific forms of dance culture amongst Asian youth, not only around funk and hip-hop music, but also around their fusion with traditional Indian dance and music forms such as Bhangra. This latter has become the site of massive popular partici- pation amongst young Asian men and women at live concerts, discos and daytime events.

In recent years, there has been something of a diversification in music policy in some city-centre entertainment networks. In order to stay in business many clubs and discos have had to hire out their facilities to one-off 'specialist' agents, or open their doors to par- ticular musical taste groups (punk/new wave, heavy metal, soul/ funk, reggae) on particular nights of the week. One consequence of this change in policy is that club goers and DJs have been able to create their own musical and stylistic categories and admission policies.

The more serious young dancers invest considerable work and training in their dancing routines. Two young Afro-Caribbean dancers from Walsall, for example, spoke about how they had learnt to breakdance by practising to a drum machine at home in front of a mirror:

A lot of us train before we come out of the house, don't we? I always do. If I know I'm on tonight I'm always stretching in the day. I always stretch every day, bend your back up and every- thing, handstand against the wall. You have to loosen your arms and loosen your body first and you've got to move your arms up and across sort of thing, and get it down your body.

(*Ignition/Young at Art*, p. 14)

With their often elaborate and sophisticated moves, these more worked-up forms of popular dance have their own grounded aes- thetic criteria for those that practise them, criteria of originality, wit and flexibility. Amongst some young dance crews (informal teams of dancers) their routines had become a kind of mime with clearly apparent narratives to them:

There's a few teams, right, they're really breakers but they're mainly acting. They go on stage, they do a few dance moves but what they're actually doing is acting, there's a story behind it all. So they do a few moves and they leave the audience to fill in the rest.

(*Ignition/Young At Art*, p. 14)

These young people were perfectly sure that what they were doing
was worth something, culturally and aesthetically. To them it was
an achievement to have reached a certain level of competence and
skill in their dancing, a lasting achievement that would be remem-
bered and even handed down to subsequent generations, rather
than just a passing fad of youth. Accordingly, they felt that their
dancing was just as legitimate, and deserving of the label art, as
classical dance and ballet:

> It's a bit of an achievement. When I'm a certain age I can look
> back and say 'This is what I done' sort of thing to my son, you
> know. I've achieved something, teaching people. You can say
> when you're old, I've done all this lot and now it's your turn, so
> you live your life to a good potential, rather than going to the
> pub every day for twenty-five years or something . . . you've
> achieved something.

> Breaking's another form of dancing, like ballet is. You've got
> ballet and other types of dancing. Bodypopping is dancing, isn't
> it?
>   (*Ignition/Young at Art*, p. 14)

Whereas dancing used to be seen as something of a feminine
activity by some working-class young men, it has become more
acceptable for males to express themselves through body movement. Some of the ties between dance forms and codes of masculin-
ity/feminity have been loosened. They still remain however. A
double cultural standard proscribes female participation in the
more acrobatic, male-defined moves or links them unfavourably to
masculine images.

For the young unemployed dancer there may be some connection
here between the grounded aesthetic of power and bodily control
exercised in dance and the predicament of worklessness. Besides
being an alternative way of filling in time, 'working' and controlling the body might be some kind of consolation for the shrinking
sense of power and control experienced elsewhere. Dancing, at this
level, affords a sense of personal power, energy and control through
bodily movement and the flaunting of a unique style which can
provide some kind of displaced resolution to the powerlessness of
the dole.

Interpreting songs and symbols

Many young people have a strong investment in the lyrical themes,
imagery and symbolism of popular music. Some young people

acquire an intimate and considerable knowledge of the semantic complexities and nuances of song lyrics, a knowledge gleaned from close listening, perhaps in the privacy of a bedroom, and from the scrutiny of lyrics printed on album covers.

In many respects, popular music still chronicles the feelings and life experiences of large sections of young people, providing a medium through which an affective grounded aesthetic can be developed to enable personal and private feelings to be expressed and shared. Pop songs provide young listeners with a set of public discourses (about emotional or romantic relationships, for example) which both play back to people their own situations and experiences, and provide a means of interpreting those experiences. Young people use song narratives to make sense of their everyday conditions of existence, and particularly the experience of growing up. Many pop lyrics help in this by working on everyday, ordinary language, and giving it a special kind of resonance, power and poetry.

Popular music can be a conversational resource. The knowledge of lyrics, styles and genres is often used as the coins of exchange in casual talk. By listening to music together and using it as a background to their lives, by expressing affiliation to particular taste groups, popular music becomes one of the principal means by which young people define themselves.

It has now become a basic axiom of popular music studies that songs are open to multiple and diverse interpretations. The metaphors and narratives of some songs can have a certain looseness of meaning which enables different readings of lyrics to be made by listeners who are differently placed, socially, and in different contexts of consumption and who are developing their own specific grounded aesthetics. The appeal of any particular song might not depend on its literally making sense, but on its susceptibility to selective interpretation. Some young people may hear and use only certain fragments of lyrics, particular stanzas or lines which have some personal resonance, and which can be extrapolated from the general context of a song.

A lot depends, here, on the linguistic codes and terms of address used in songs. The pronouns of 'I', 'we', 'they' and 'you' used in lyrics, for example, can be made applicable to different situations and different senses of identity. This is one way that popular music forms and genres work to put together an audience, or a particular 'community', to construct a sense of 'us' and 'them'. But the preponderance of these terms of address in popular music allows listeners to impose their own identities on a song. You can read yourself into a song, and temporarily inhabit its identities and discourses along the dynamic of a particular self-created grounded aesthetic. The sophisticated sound reproduction of the recorded voice and the conversational qualities of many popular music lyrics are further linguistic codes which can be inhabited by and so made highly personal to the listener. Songs are made somehow to really speak for the listener. As Paul, a dedicated fan of Bob Marley, points out, 'A lot of people relate to Bob Marley, and I can see why, you know, 'cause a lot of the things he sings about I've been through myself.'

Listening to music can also be an informal educative process, especially where songs deal with more explicitly political and social themes. Songs can be a source of political ideas and development when focused around particular issues, such as gender relations, war, apartheid, unemployment, nuclear weapons or ecological questions.

Many young people have a strong investment operating through a spiritual grounded aesthetic in songs which are seen to have a good meaning or a moral point to them, songs which dispense wisdom and good sense. In Jane's case, for example, referring to reggae in particular, she felt that music could be a source of spiritual nourishment:

> It's telling people something through music, through something that most people like and enjoy. It gives you a lot of wisdom. 'Cause in your heart, you know you feel that way, and when you listen to it you know that other people are thinking on them same kind of ways, and it kind of gives you more strength.

While many young people use music to situate themselves, historically and politically, through creative work with its symbolic forms and meanings, for young black people this process is especially important. Black youth have consistently found and made a political and cultural resonance in the themes and discourses of musical traditions which have their origins outside Britain, in Jamaican reggae and black American soul music, for example. What black musical forms like reggae and hip-hop make available are symbolic resources for the oppositional understanding and grounded aesthetic quickening of the otherwise wholly negative experiences of powerlessness and racial domination. Jamaican music supplies, for instance, the language and symbols of Rastafari, a whole range of anti-capitalist/racist themes, as well as a critique of the state. Black American music gives a language and imagery for the problems of urban living, of police harassment, for the problems of work, leisure, gender conflict and sexuality. The music of the black church, for its part, has also increasingly provided a set of symbolic and historical meanings for many young blacks, and a spiritual language around which an interpretive community can be created.

The eighties has seen a veritable explosion in musical activity amongst young black Britons, with more and more black music produced and recorded in Britain. It has also seen the emergence of new, syncretic, black British musical forms. These are forms that have rearticulated Caribbean and black American styles, yet whose content and character is shaped in response to specifically British circumstances, and in line with the changing expressive needs of young black people and their grounded aesthetics.

Far from being an insular culture, existing on the fringes of white society, black musical traditions have also had an important inter- pretive resource for the symbolic work of other social groups. Asian youth, for example have found a relevance in soul, funk, disco and hip-hop music, music out of which new, distinctly British, Asian youth cultural forms are being evolved. White youth too continue to find in black music a language and set of symbols with which to express their own age, gender or class-based experiences. Thus some young whites relate strongly to reggae, soul, hip-hop and rap. One young white man applied the theme of 'sufferation' (oppres- sion), used in many of Bob Marley's songs, to his own particular experience of school:

> I could relate very strongly to 'sufferation' and sufferers' music, even though I wasn't black . . . you know, 'Stop pushing me, Mr Boss Man', loads of songs . . . And the ones about freedom too. 'Cause I hated school, I felt I was captive by school, and by people in authority.

Popular music is always listened to within specific social settings and locations, and used as a background to any number of activities, from courting and sexual encounters, dancing in clubs, to surviving in work, or defeating boredom in the home. Music is also used to create and mark off physical and cultural space as young people's space, be it in the bedroom, the disco, the youth club, shopping precinct, street, park or concert hall. It is through these situated contexts of consumption that specific grounded aesthetics are given shape and activated and which in turn connect different sites and practices so that 'private' listening also benefits from the collective effervescence of the dance-floor.

Consumption into production

Sound systems

Most young people's musical activities are largely centred around recorded music. It is often the more avid young record collectors and taste leaders who provide the musical entertainment at young people's informal leisure institutions, be they parties or discos. This is a common way in which some young people become DJs, or start their own discos – a crucial and interesting point where grounded aesthetics begin to produce the more formal and public in a specific attempt to reflect or induce, promote or enable the grounded aesthetics of others or of collectiveness. A particularly heightened example of this public use of recorded music is the institution of the sound system amongst young Afro-Caribbeans, an institution where the activities of consumption merge into and become intertwined with more conventional forms of production.

Besides being one of the principal focal points of musical activity within the black community, the sound system also involves a number of primary private production processes, which embrace electronics, sound technology and carpentry. These informal processes are motivated by specifically musical enthusiasms and operate to their own cultural agenda. They often involve the use of independently gained technical knowledge and skills, picked up from electronics magazines.

In this process the mainstream domestic hi-fi equipment is raided for technical ideas which are then incorporated into the workings of the sound system. Commercially available sound equipment and technology are personalized and humanized; turntables and amplifiers, for example, are customized, while speaker boxes are designed and purpose built to house the large 18-in. bass speakers used by sound systems.

Sound systems not only provide a crucial promotional and broadcasting outlet for black music, particularly reggae, but also function as a key site of commercial self-activity amongst young black people. The larger and more successful sounds have a very real economic rationale, generating income from the sale of food and drink and from cover charges at dances and parties. Sound systems are one of the key institutions in an autonomous commercial infrastructure for the independent production, distribution and retail of black music. Many of these enterprises have been owned and run by black people themselves and sustained to a large degree through purchasing power within the black community. They form the lynchpin in what amounts to an alternative, local entertainment industry, comprised of recording studios, labels, night clubs, sound systems/discos, record shops, boutiques and pirate radio stations.

As consumers and producers, black youth have suffered persistent discrimination from mainstream commercial leisure institutions which have actively excluded them or failed to cater for their musical tastes. The community's cultural and leisure activities have historically been the object of state harassment and suppression. Indeed, it is partly in response to such exclusion that the black community as a whole has been forced to build its own alternative leisure spaces out of a network of private houses, night clubs, and municipal buildings. The irony here perhaps is that young black people's musical activity is often the *result* of their powerlessness, their disenfranchisement and marginalization by the mainstream leisure industry. It is out of that predicament that young blacks, whether as consumers or musicians, carve collective space for themselves and develop an infrastructure of street-level economic enterprises and institutions.

Sound systems, then, are valuable cultural resources for the black community as a whole, and invested with considerable symbolic importance. As one sound system operator pointed out, they provide:

> Entertainment ... Somewhere to go on a weekend, for us anyway – black people. We don't go to football matches, we don't go to the pub, so we go a dance ... We play music to suit the occasion ... Our aim is directly to play to entertain the crowd 'cause that's what we get pay for.
>
> (*Black Echoes*, 11 August 1984)

In some urban areas where young whites face the same lack of finances, transport and leisure options as their black peers, they can become alternative leisure institutions for white youth too. As one young white informant says:

> When you've been there a year on the dole, and all your friends are still there, everything starts to slot into place, you know what I mean? ... Because if you're on the dole, you can't really afford to go the night clubs up town. And like goin' blues is one of the few things you can.

For other young whites, blues parties and sound-system dances were an alternative to mainstream and official provision for the young in the white community, whether in the form of youth clubs or commercial discos. The lack of dress restrictions, the hours of operation and the cultural practices of sound-system-based events were all seen as preferable to the more regulated and depersonalized forms of leisure provided by mainstream commercial discos. For unemployed young whites as well as young blacks, the sound system could be one kind of solution to their exclusion from mainstream, and particularly city-centre leisure spaces.

Black music and oral poetry

The grounded aesthetics of a sound-system dance or a party divest records of their status as artistic statements with fixed meanings. New meanings are attached to them. Transmitted through the sound system and consumed by the audience at a distance from their initial context of production, they undergo a series of symbolic and material transformations. These include the creativity of the actual selection and ordering of music; the processing of the music itself by a whole battery of technological hardware, including equalizers, echo chambers, digital delay units, mixing desks and effects boxes; the use of records and turntables as percussive devices as in 'scratching' – thrusting a record back and forth while the needle is still in the groove; the cutting and mixing of fragments of different records into one another, using multiple turntables. These characteristic rituals of performance help to socialize the experience of dancing to recorded music, turning it into a creative performance and an event. Of all these practices, perhaps the most important are the improvised forms of oral poetry of DJ-ing, toasting and rapping.

In the live context it is the DJ or MC (mike chanter) who introduces the music, delivers improvised lyrics to the crowd and directs the dance as a whole with various interjections and exhortations. The grounded aesthetics here, or one of them, is to link words, poetic rhymes and statements together in time to the music's rhythms, and to improvise narratives of a topical nature.

DJ-ing is, in fact, a popular form of oral poetry which appropriates discourses and styles of commercially available reggae music but which also grows out of the everyday situations, their dramatic grounded aesthetics, their language and vocabulary. The art of the DJ is a more worked-up form of that language, with DJs delivering their narratives and observations in the popular vernacular of the street. DJ lyrics offer highly articulate commentaries on any number of social, economic and political issues and are increasingly addressed to the peculiarities of everyday life in Britain for young black people.

For all DJs, the live atmosphere of a dance is a crucial source of inspiration and symbolic creativity. Kojak and Flux, two DJs for a local Birmingham sound system, spoke of how they would absorb the 'vibes' of a live event, drawing inspiration from the audience, from other DJs or from a particular record. As Flux explains:

F: Well what usually happen is . . . the sound is playing, right, and you ketch a lickle vibes for y'self, you know . . . or someone crack a joke . . . You know what I mean?

K: Like, most people, right, they would work off a record as well. You know, certain record can give you that little vibes, too, you know, and you can just work 'pon it.

Forms of symbolic work in DJ-ing differ. Kojak describes himself as a 'head top' DJ, because he tends to improvise lyrics straight off the top of his head in a dance or blues and set a mood with a certain style and humour, rather than 'chatting' in a more self-conscious and structured way with lyrics about a specific subject. Flux, alternatively, used a more structured set of lyrics and verbal routines which he wrote down and carefully rehearsed. Flux, like many DJs, writes down his lyrics in a diary that he carries with him every day, making entries as ideas come to him. Flux describes how he would improvise around a given topic, trying to match up rhyming couplets:

Me start off with a description of everything me could think about this certain thing. Like say you're talking 'bout a car . . . you talk 'bout what mek up de car, which factory de car come from, how much nut and bolt it have . . . this and that, and then you try to make it all fit, you know what I mean.

A similar creative adaptation of black American musical styles, images and oral forms has occurred since 1984 in the area of hip-hop and rap. While British rap was initially imitative of American genres, it has developed into a distinctly black British form of oral poetry. Like reggae DJ-ing, such poetry and its grounded aesthetics emerge out of simple everyday observations couched in idioms and expressions that are drawn from American rap records, as well as from Black British English. As two young rappers from Wednesbury stated:

T: We rap about ourselves, about the scene, what's going on.

D: I rap about my mom's food, life at college and my mates and you know, girls, about the teachers . . . You know, things like that.

T: Sex, money, drugs, robberies, things like that, things happening every day.

D: You can say what comes in to your head really, but if you keep repeating everything they get boring.

(*Ignition/Young at Art*, pp. 8–9)

Many rappers and DJs rehearse their lyrics by rapping to the rhythm
of a drum machine, taping their voices and then going back over
their lyrics, tightening and polishing them up. Since 1985/6 scores
of British rap crews have emerged, using American idioms as a
springboard for their own characteristic styles of delivery.

While rapping, like reggae DJ-ing, still remains something of a
male-dominated practice, young women DJs and rap crews have
nevertheless begun to emerge, drawing inspiration for their symbolic creativity from American female rap groups like Salt 'n' Pepa
and bringing their own distinctively female style and humour to
bear on the rapping tradition. As a member of the She Rockers, one
of the most successful of recent British female rap crews, pointed
out:

> Lyrically, no one can touch us, and that's kind of unusual for
> girls. Before Salt 'n' Pepa all the girls featured on rap records
> were very soft, like token females. We don't portray ourselves
> as hard, we just say what we have to say. We don't allow the
> fact that we're girls to stop us from doing anything . . . We
> promote women as decent, respectable people; not as objects of
> sex or ridicule; promoting women as just as good as any man.
>
>   (*Soul Underground*, March 1988, p. 15)

While the boom in rap has opened some doors in the music
industry to young black and white people, many practitioners
remain highly protective of their skills, caught in the contradiction
between wanting due reward for their achievements, yet wary of
those achievements being robbed of their vitality and ripped out of
their cultural context by the media.

In 1984/5, for example, the mainstream media latched on to
hip-hop, with videos, advertisements, hoardings and radio jingles
using hip-hop-style graphics, rap and breakdancing. It was a process
not without some resistance, however, amongst some involved in
the rap/hip-hop scene. One young female rapper had this to say
about the hip-hop bandwagon in the media:

> I think they're spoiling it, really squeezing everything out of it.
> We're trying to keep away from all that. We've got our own
> nations and we're having our own thing. It's our world, our
> hip-hop world, and I'm not going to let them destroy it like
> they did everything else.
>
>   (*City Limits*, 17–23 May 1985)

DIY recording and mixing

Since the early eighties, a number of developments at the bottom
end of the domestic hi-fi and recording technology markets have

revolutionized the potentials for the symbolic creativity of young people in music and greatly increased the possibilities of music-making, particularly around the practices of mixing, sampling, bootlegging and home recording. These have emerged partly from the popular practices of home taping and recording mentioned above, and partly from the influences of black American dance music and hip-hop culture. They have enabled a process of the more formal reflection of grounded aesthetics in a 'bottom-end-up' process of promoting the grounded aesthetics of wider groups and collectivities.

With two turntables, a cassette recorder and skilful use of pause buttons, switches and faders, it is possible to mix tapes and create cut-ups for circulation amongst friends. In this process the hardware and software of *consumption* have become the instruments and the raw materials of a kind of cultural production. For many, this is for the simple reason that they are cheaper to buy, and easier to learn to play than expensive musical instruments.

Some of this home-made music never finds its way on to vinyl or into a formal stage show. It is distributed solely on tape and heard at mobile clubs, house parties and dances.

Mixing offers young people who can't play instruments a way of making music. Recorded music becomes the source material for the creation of a completely new piece which can claim its own validity. In this way, young DJs or mixers can become 'artists' in their own right, questioning conventional notions of musical skill and undermining some of the established rules of musical composition and authorship.

This kind of bootleg mixing has been considerably aided by the introduction of sampling devices which enable sounds to be collected from a variety of sources, whether records, TV programmes or the radio, and then overdubbed on a custom-built dance rhythm obtained from a drum machine. The specific grounded aesthetic here, as one DJ pointed out, is increasingly one of 'technical skill and imagination on two turntables with any record, whether it's electro, classical, new wave, rock, whatever. It's the way you actually use it, and not the record itself that's important.' Sampling, as one young studio operator said in Birmingham was 'the only way to do it', when it came to recording and mixing:

> I pinch a lot of my material straight off other people's records
> ... You know, whereas someone like Sly Dunbar [famous reggae session drummer] will have spent ten hours trying to get the right sound for his drum kit, it's pointless me spending that

same time to try and recreate that, when I can actually lift it
straight off his record with a sampler.

With the falling costs of recording equipment like drum machines,
sequencers, samplers and keyboards, it is now possible to make
records of high quality entirely within one's front room.

DIY-recorded British soul, reggae and house music is now being
produced out of a growing network of small studios which have
sprung up in virtually every major urban area of Britain. In many
such studios, few instruments are used at all. Rhythm tracks are
created by selecting sounds from a bank of synthesizers, keyboards
and drum machines, the operations of which are accessed and
programmed through a computer. Paul, for example, has his own
studio in Birmingham where he records local singers who simply
'voice over' rhythm tracks that he has made himself. For Paul,
writing a dance song is more like a process of building, adding layer
upon layer of different sounds, musical textures and rhythms:

> I start with a drum pattern, to give it the feel of it, and I play the
> chords to the drum pattern, so you can sing along, and get the
> rhythm kind of thing. Then I'll programme a bass line, which
> will interact with the drum pattern or the vocals . . . And once
> you've got the basic groove going, then you go into the finer
> details, sort of thing, sort of sparkly bits, just to make it work.

As record companies have begun to see its commercial potential, an
increasing amount of this DIY dance music is being recorded and
released, occasionally through the majors, but more often than not
on small independent labels. Promoted and distributed outside
mainstream music-industry channels, for example through pirate
radio, specialist record shops or particular clubs and dances, such
music has come to occupy an increasingly large part of young
people's listening.

Music-making and performance

There is now a long and well-established performing tradition of
instrumental and vocal music-making amongst young people, practices which embody grounded aesthetics and reflect and promote
their possibilities in others somehow sharing the same symbolic
community. Recent studies suggest that, today, the practice of
music-making amongst the young is as extensive as ever.[2] A 1980
survey of young music-makers in Liverpool, for example, noted
that there were more than a thousand bands on Merseyside alone.
But how do young people become interested in music-making?

What kinds of cultural practices and informal arrangements do young musicians themselves evolve, and what aesthetic criteria do they use for critically judging what they do?

Young people's interest in music-making and performance invariably begins from their activities as consumers, fans and dancers, and from the grounded aesthetics and pleasures of listening to and liking particular styles of music. For example, Kevin's interest in music-making came about as an extension of listening to records, dancing in night clubs and being inspired by his favourite bands:

> I've always been interested in music. I've got loads of records, I always did buy music, and I used to dance a lot . . . That's got a lot to do with it you see . . . So the music was just an extension of that, 'cause I always wanted to know, you know, how they did it, or what they did to make people move sort of thing . . . So then I started experimenting, started doing things with music, just messing about . . .

Kevin subsequently bought a synthesizer and learnt to play it by trying to copy his favourite records:

> The funny thing about it, was the sounds that they were using were similar to the sounds I was getting on the machine. So I thought that's amazing! I can actually *do* it, you know. And once you can actually play along with the melody, and work it out, it's just so good, you know what I mean?

The sense of empowerment achieved by being able to play an instrument and reproduce the sounds of a favourite record is a common starting point for young musicians. To learn by copying and experimenting (the usual mode for young rock musicians) is necessarily to be inventive. Guitarists, drummers and keyboard players have to work out how to sound like their role models, usually with quite different (and much cheaper) sound equipment. This means developing manual and technical skills, a discriminating ear, and an *ad hoc* understanding of sound amplification. As Kevin points out:

> I was never taught or anything. Everything I do is by ear . . . it's all what I feel or what I've heard. I mean some people I know, they've been taught and all that, and they're really good sort of thing, but they can't improvise, they find it difficult to sort of, you know, do anything themselves, rather than sort of have a piece of music in front of them, and playing it.

While Kevin eventually went on to teach himself to read music, many young people learn to play musical instruments from DIY teach-yourself manuals, or from sheet music, both now stocked in considerable quantities by most high-street bookshops.

Amongst young rock musicians, there is usually a short gap between picking up an instrument and playing in a band, and the learning process is as much a result of practising, rehearsing and jamming together as it is of any prior, individual training and skill acquisition. Most rock bands compose their own music through informal musical procedures, procedures which bring into play grounded aesthetics to indicate what sounds good, and how to generate an effect. Because rock musicians don't read music, they have to learn to play together in endless collective experiments, through hours spent rehearsing together. In Kevin's band, for example, song-writing invariably evolved out of such improvised jamming sessions:

> Usually, we'd just jam, then if we'd get a really nice section, we'd sort of say 'Oh, that was good, let's try that again, we'll do that twice' and then we'd do that part, and cut other bits out, and try and string it together like. And as for words, and stuff like that, it wasn't sort of a session where everyone was sort of sat round, and sort of writ a song. It was more like 'Eh, try singing this, this sounds all right!' or 'Try this,' you know what I mean, so it was just done there and then sort of thing.

Though there's an obvious interest in trying to improve the performance as the vehicle, the impulse to embody grounded aesthetics more formally for public expression is driven by the aim to reflect and promote grounded aesthetics in a wider community – not by the attempt to produce perfect 'things'.

For virtually all young rock bands, live performance is the focal point of their work. As many young musicians explain, it is in performance that they experience the most intense feelings of achievement. To be on stage is to be the object of public attention, and to have the glamour of their chosen musical role confirmed. Kevin felt that each one of the gigs that they'd played live was a great occasion: 'It was all really good. 'Cause we was all young, and really into the idea of "the band", kind of thing, and everything was for "the band", and we were all together, like . . . we just had a really good time.'

The pleasures of playing music together, collectively, or just 'having a good time' are paramount for young musicians. Most repeatedly stress the comradeship of playing together in a band, the excitement of being on stage, of giving people pleasure and excitement, of getting some public recognition and using music as an outlet for creative energy and expertise.

> When I first started out, it was like, being, you know, with loads of your mates, making music and going and playing, in the hope that one day, something really good's gonna come out of it . . . You've always got that kind of . . . hope . . . of doing something really good, when you stand up and sing, on a big stage . . . It's sort of like that . . . We had really high hopes.

While almost all young rock musicians do fantasize about 'making it' nationally and dream about the selfish rewards and releases of power and money, and though many take the first steps to achieve this by making demo tapes for radio play and record company attention, the most immediate reasons bands keep going are local support and appreciation. Playing music, moreover, is only one role in a more elaborate set of tasks and relationships, involving a support network of helpers, entrepreneurs, promoters and publicists, drivers and carriers, collectors, fans and followers. A performing pop band depends on a lot of people undertaking different tasks, using their own organizational and entrepreneurial, as well as musical, skills.

Musical performance, then, in this wider sense, amounts to an important expression and celebration of sociability enabled through some shared sense of grounded aesthetics. It is inherently a collective activity. Musicians know that personal fulfilment depends on the ability to do things together, whether learning to listen, and adjust, to other players in the band, or evolving informal attempts at collective organization, decision-making and financial management. For example they club together to buy equipment or hold regular band meetings. In describing performance as their most satisfying musical experience, young musicians are describing a kind of collective experience which involves the audience too. When a rock show works, it is because, in speaking to the crowd, the musicians come to speak for them: the music both creates and articulates the very idea of a symbolically creative community.

For large numbers of unemployed young people, music-making may assume a special kind of importance in a context where the priorities are those of day-to-day economic survival, independence from state control and the use and meaning of leisure. For them, music-related activities can function as important sources of cultural self-sufficiency through which to negotiate the boredom of the dole and survive the disorientation of worklessness. Music-making enables some unemployed young to develop grounded aesthetics which provide a cultural and psychological defence mechanism against the dispiriting effects of unemployment on their everyday lives.

Ironically, the dole, particularly since the punk era, has been one of the principal unofficial funders of musical activity amongst the young, by providing at least some space and financial security for young musicians. The shared predicament of unemployment continues to supply a common denominator of experience for many young bands, providing a focal point for shared musical enthusiasms, for symbolic creativity and, often, political values. In the West Midlands, for example, music-making has long been a site in which musicians from different communities and backgrounds have intermixed and exchanged traditions.

This chapter has illustrated how the usually separately understood processes of musical production and consumption are closely related. The distinctions between them are blurred in musical practice, particularly around new musical technologies of consumption and production, and new symbolic uses of commodities. Consumption is itself a kind of self-creation – of identities, of space, of cultural forms – with its own kinds of cultural empowerment.

These forms of creative consumption around popular music point to a continuum between the more worked-up forms of musical activity and the popular practices engaged in by the young. If it's more 'producers' we want, then instead of concentrating on identifying and promoting creative élites or potential élites, we should, instead, focus on a general lubrication of the connections between these everyday forms of musical and cultural activity and the more formally recognized practices, to make the passage from the role of 'consumer' to that of 'producer' easier.

But most crucially it is the symbolic creativity pervading *all* musical practices which we wish to emphasize. Grounded aesthetics developed here are essential to the ways in which young people make sense of the social world and their place within it. Music, in short, is not just something young people like and do. It is in many ways the model for their involvement in a common culture which provides the resources to see beyond the immediate requirements and contradictions of work, family and the dole. It is this widest symbolic creativity which should be recognized and promoted in the provision of the general conditions and spaces that can allow young people's musical practices to flourish – to create the supportive environmental, economic and social conditions which enable them to do better and more creatively what they do already.

Notes

1 Simon Jones, *Black Culture, White Youth*, Macmillan, 1988.
2 See R. Finnegan, *The Practice of Music*, CUP, 1989; S. Cohen, *Society and Culture on The Making of Rock Music in Liverpool*. D. Phil, Oxford, 1987.

— 4 —
Style, fashion and symbolic creativity

Like high art and classical music, the world of couture fashion design has its own autonomous, élite tradition which explains itself according to the creative innovations of individual 'great men'. The exclusive products of the few top designers are comparable in financial terms to the posthumous works of great artists. Reproduction of these exclusive garments filters down selectively to mass-production level, mediated and reinterpreted by the fashion press, in-house department stores and designers, or reproduced cheaply by small fashion manufacturers.

The scenario is one in which fashion ideas initiated in Paris, Milan or New York are in some mediated form felt, seen and bought in department stores throughout the world. In this world a few significant shapes dominate the season and are changed according to the needs and purses of the social élite.

Couture, however, has historically only ever been a small part of the fashion industry, not its apex. Fashion designers have played a much less central role in setting fashion trends than is commonly imagined. Since World War I Britain's textile and garment industry has been progressively diminished parallel to a massive expansion in the popular retail trade in ready-to-wear clothing. The post-war period and the 1960s in particular marked the beginning of a new phase in the mass consumption of clothes, marked by a convergence of innovative design, youth fashion and the invention of synthetic fibres, under the conditions of full employment and increased spending. This convergence of influences helped overturn the previous international trickle-down effect in fashion, allowing a certain democratization of style and fashion that undermined the centrality of the designers.

The expansion in the high-street consumption of clothes has continued apace in the 1980s, the most significant development

h of the middle-market fashion industry, making
ion clothes accessible to more people through
, Principles and Burtons. Behind the altered look of
however, lies another set of equally significant
lar fashion, clothing and consumption patterns –
tylistic creativity from below.
e and fashion have long been recognized as key
ng people's expression, exploration and making of
ividual and collective identities. They remain
st visible forms of symbolic cultural creativity and
y in people's lives in our common culture. As in
other areas we have looked at, there is here a specific grounded
aesthetic dynamic even in apparently passive consumption which
stretches into and lies on a continuum with more obviously
creative activities. We try to spell out some of this.

In presenting these forms of informal symbolic work this chapter
draws from fieldwork in Wolverhampton and Birmingham and, in
the case of the hairstyle section, London.

Clothes and creative consumption

Clothes shopping has been a central part of post-war youth cultural
consumerism. As a cultural practice, however, shopping has tended
to be marginalized in much of the writing about youth, style and
fashion. Shopping has been considered a private and feminine
activity and part of the process of incorporation into the social
machinery.

But young people don't just buy passively or uncritically. They
always transform the meaning of bought goods, appropriating and
recontextualizing mass-market styles. That appropriation entails a
form of symbolic work and creativity as young consumers break the
ordered categories of clothes, the suggested matches and ideas
promoted by shops. They bring their own specific and differentiated
grounded aesthetics to bear on consumption, choosing their own
colours and matches and personalizing their purchases. Most
young people combine elements of clothing to create new meanings. They adopt and adapt clothing items drawn from government
surplus stores, for example, or training shoes, track suits, rugby
shirts, Fred Perry tops from sportswear shops. They make their own
sense of what is commercially available, make their own aesthetic
judgements, and sometimes reject the normative definitions and
categories of 'fashion' promoted by the clothing industry.

While many of the young people we spoke to obtain their ideas
about clothes from friends or from simply observing how clothes

looked worn on other people, many also use the media to understand and keep up with the latest fashions. They get ideas about
clothes from sources such as television programmes, like *The
Clothes Show*, fashion and music magazines, or from the personal
dress styles of particular pop artists. Aspects of the clothes and
outfits worn by pop groups like Bananarama and Amazulu, for
example, were taken up *en masse* by young women in the early
and mid-1980s, particularly items such as haystack hairstyles,
dungarees and children's plimsolls.

Since the early 1980s, media and marketing attention has shifted
towards the employed with high salaries such as the 25–40 age
group and the 'empty-nesters'. Changing economic circumstances,
particularly the growth in youth unemployment and the start of
what will be a long-term decline in the youth population, have
made the 16-to-24-year-old market far less attractive and lucrative.
This has meant that there now exists a substantial block of young
people for whom the retail boom has provided few benefits. With
many working-class youth now denied the sources of income
which financed the spectacular subcultures of the 1960s and 1970s,
the right to 'good clothes' can no longer be automatically assumed.

The young unemployed especially find it difficult to develop
their own image and life style through purchased items. For these
young people, using clothes to express their identities, stylistically,
is something of a luxury. With social identities increasingly defined
in terms of the capacity for private, individualized consumption,
those who are excluded from that consumption feel frustrated and
alienated.

For many working-class young people impotent window shopping is a source of immense frustration. One young woman said
that she would not go window shopping for this reason:

> I don't like window shopping very much. Especially if I don't
> have the money . . . 'cause if you see something and you want
> it, you can't afford it. So I don't go window shopping unless I
> have money.

Remarkably, however, even young people with limited spending
power still often find ways to dress stylishly and to express their
identities through the clothes they wear. Young women and men
still manage to dress smartly and make the most out of slender
resources, buying secondhand clothes or saving up to buy particular
items of clothing. For some the emphasis on presenting a smart or
fashionable image is a priority above everything else and results in
quite disproportionate amounts being spent on clothes. One young
woman said that she bought a clothing item every week, but

sacrificed by going 'skint' for the rest of the week. Her rationale was that quality was better than quantity:

> I'd rather buy things that'll last me than cheap things what won't, and you don't get the quality in them, do you? . . . I feel better in myself if I know I've got summat on like expensive, instead of cheap.

From subculture to 'retro'

The succession of spectacular youth subcultures has shown particular, conspicuous, symbolic creativity in clothes. There is now a long and well-known list of youth subcultural styles, from the teddy boys and the mods, to the skins and punks, which have occupied the attention of sociologists, journalists and fashion commentators alike. The distinct styles of post-war youth subcultures have been interpreted as symbolic solutions to age and class domination, and a means of marking out and winning cultural space for young people. Such styles have been lauded for their symbolic work in borrowing and transforming everyday objects or fashion components, recoding them according to internal subcultural grounded aesthetics. Examples include the teds' appropriation of the Edwardian suit, the skins' appropriation of proletarian work clothes, or the punks' borrowing of safety pins, bin liners and zips.

While only a small minority of young people adopted the complete uniform of youth subcultures, large numbers drew on selective elements of their styles creating their own meanings and uses from them. Many subcultural styles became popularized, finding their way into mainstream working-class and middle-class youth culture. In this way, subcultures became a source of inspiration for the stylistic symbolic work and creativity of all young people. Punk, for example, stimulated a move back to straight-legged trousers, smaller collars and shorter hair amongst young people of all ages. The leggings/thermal underpants first worn by punk girls – which were originally cream and had to be dyed black – were soon being made up new by young market-stall holders. By the summer of 1985 they were being produced in T-shirt cotton and a wide range of colours and had become a definitive fashion item for all women under the age of 40.

But fashion trends arise not only from the street – though always in a dialectic with it. Punk, for example, emanated as much from the art-school avant-garde as it did from the dance halls and housing estates. Many of the stylistic innovators in punk had a firm stake in the commodity market themselves. Indeed, within most post-war

youth subcultures, young people have always been directly involved in the production and selling of clothes themselves. A whole
economic infrastructure of entrepreneurial activity has accompanied all the major post-war youth style explosions, creating careers
for many of those involved.

Punk was perhaps the last major subculture in which there was a
convergence of design, subcultural style and small innovative retail
businesses. Malcolm McLaren and Vivienne Westwood's shop 'Sex'
(later renamed 'Seditionaries'), set up in the Kings Road in the
mid-70s, was one of the few which integrated popular street fashion
with the music of the time.

Since punk the stylistic options among an increasingly self-
reflexive and stylistically mobile youth have been greatly expanded
with revivals of all the major subcultures occurring in the late
1970s and '80s. Punk itself reproduced the entire sartorial history of
post-war working-class youth culture in cut-up form, combining
elements which had originally belonged to completely different
epochs. The wardrobes of past subcultural styles were exhumed,
re-adapted and recombined in endlessly different combinations.

Since and including the punk explosion, then, one of the most
important trends in youth style has been the rehabilitation and
raiding of previous sartorial styles for raw material in young people's own, current symbolic work and creativity, stylistic and
cultural expression. Retro style is part of a general trend in contemporary culture which ransacks various historical moments for their
key stylistic expressions and then re-inserts and recombines them
in current fashion. Clothing items are worn as though in quotation
marks, their wearers self-consciously evoking some past, even at
the risk of stylistic mismatch and incongruity. These references to
past stylistic forms have taken on a kind of iconographic status in
pop culture, evoking whole periods of social history, and have been
used extensively in popular music and advertising.

Clothes and identity

Clothes, like musical tastes, are an indication of the cultural
identities and leisure orientations of different groups of young
people. Young people are very adept at the symbolic work of
developing their own styles and also at 'reading off' and decoding
the dress styles of others and relating them to musical, political and
social orientations. Thus, as one young woman noted, people who
liked 'house music', dressed in the 'house style' – Dr Martens
shoes/boots, scarves, baggy shirts, old checked jackets with long
collars, baggy trousers – 'things that don't fit you, but look smart.'

But clothes signify more than just musical tastes. No longer are they an automatic reflection of subcultural affiliations or collective social identities. Clothes are also a crucial medium for grounded aesthetics in which young people express and explore their own specific individual identities. Young people learn about their inner selves partly by developing their outer image through clothes. They use style in their symbolic work to express and develop their understanding of themselves as unique persons, to signify who they are, and who they think they are. As one young woman put it, 'If I find something I know I like, if I know I like certain clothes, then I know I'm that kind of person.'

Young people's uses and choices of clothes also involve an active process of conscious, purposeful image-making. Clothes can be used playfully for the sheer pleasure of putting together a costume, or fabricating an identity. As one young woman says:

> To me, what you wear in a morning and what you wear to go out is a fancy dress, that's all I see it as because you enjoy the clothes you wear, right? . . . To me, fancy dress is everyday clothes, what you wear to college, go out to work or whatever, or what you wear to go out, it is fancy-dress costume . . . I mean, you've got a costume on now, haven't you? I've got a costume on, everybody's got a costume on . . .

Clothes can make people feel differently in different contexts. For some young people, and especially young women, the clothes they wear on any particular day will influence the way they talk, behave and present themselves. Wearing smart clothes can inspire confidence or may make some young people feel dignified or even snobbish. Wearing trousers, jeans or T-shirts was equated by others with 'being yourself', while wearing more feminine, 'going out' clothes could be equated with feeling sexy or flirtatious. Clothes can be manipulated to produce the right effect, to induce the right feeling and mood, involving subtle dressing strategies and choices of colours and styles.

Young people make clear distinctions between everyday clothes for college or work, and clothes for going out. They are used symbolically to mark the boundaries between leisure and work. Dressing to go out at night or at the weekend is an important activity which involves symbolic work and specific pleasures all of its own. Clothes are absolutely central in courtship rituals amongst young people. They are used not only to attract the opposite sex, but also to gain friends, win peer-group acceptance, and to appear different or interesting. Young people frequently put on identities when they go out, a process which includes not only dressing-up but also role-playing and putting on different accents. In a grounded aesthetic of the masque Joan, for example, reports that she wants to look different and to have people think that she is different when she goes out. She wanted to show a different side of her personality to that in college, which involved her talking and dressing differently:

> You don't want to look the same all day, do you, you want to look totally different when you go out at night . . . When I go out, they don't recognize me, because I am totally dressed up, and they think that isn't Joan, when they look at you good and proper, they think, 'God, you look totally different', and that's what you want, you don't want to look the same when you go out.

Dressing appropriately for different social contexts involves its own symbolic work, careful thought and preparation. It is something young people learn by closely scrutinizing how others dress and involves modulating one's dress to fit with different kinds of people in different contexts. As Joan points out:

> If I go to a friend's party, I think, 'What can I wear?' You know you might take out all your wardrobe just to think, I wanna wear this, I wanna wear that. But really you've got to think of the people there and what they're like. And you've got to think of their dress. You know, some of them might go in trousers, or skirts and blouses . . . You can't go in your best suits and, when you go there, people are in trousers, because you'll feel like a right fool. I've done it before and I really felt awful.

Fashion and gender

While all young people use fashion as a means of making and expressing their identities, young women invest more in working on appearance than young men. Appearance is a key means by which women not only express their individual identities and independence, but are simultaneously constituted as objects of, and for, male desire. For young women, making oneself attractive can be a tricky business since appearance can provide the basis of a young woman's reputation. It requires that young women tread the precarious line between discreet and glamorous femininity, that they sexualize their appearance but not too much. One young woman said that her boyfriend liked her to dress in a particular way when with him, but that she liked to dress differently when with her female friends:

My boyfriend wants me to dress in a skirt all the time, but when I go out with my friends, I usually wear jeans or summat, he don't like me wearing jeans and stuff like that . . . He's square . . . if I'm going out with my boyfriend, he doesn't like me looking trendy, so when I'm with my friends I like to look trendy, but he doesn't like me looking a tart or anything, he likes me in normal going-out clothes, like jeans and high heels or a long skirt, you know. Not wearing too much make-up.

Since more is at stake for young women than for young men in the realm of fashion, it is not surprising that they embellish it with such rich significance. But young women do not dress for men alone. They also dress for themselves and each other. Particular clothing styles may be used by young women to inspire confidence. Equally for young men style and clothing can be just as much about social esteem as sexual attractiveness. For some it is a considerable investment in a particular kind of masculine narcissistic display: looking 'cool'. It's a strategy of which young women are only too well aware, as one young woman pointed out:

They dress to impress us women . . . Some of the guys come in [the college] in gold sovereigns, gold necklaces, smart trousers a little way out, jackets and things like that, then they are just waiting for you to say, 'Why, you look nice,' you know what I mean? I mean, fair enough, there's times when I've done that, but I knew that was what they were waiting for.

The forms and definitions of femininity and masculinity in style and fashion are continually changing. Subtle pressures are exerted on young people to dress in particular ways by the clothing industry through models, fashion magazines, catalogues and shop layouts. However, this not only involves pressures to dress as masculine men and feminine women, but can also involve adopting styles hitherto seen as confined to the opposite sex. Here, a certain amount of unisex clothing is officially provided by some shops and marketed as such, but young women in particular also do their informal cross-gender buying of men's clothes. Some young women felt that men's clothes were nicer than women's and had more style. One young woman said that she bought men's clothes because, 'they're baggy, comfortable' and 'have a lot of wear in them'. The larger size and baggier look of men's clothes make them suitable for all female sizes and shapes, allowing a more democratic fashion open to all young women. As consumers, young women have consistently broken down some of the gender categories used in shops, despite retailers' attempts rigidly to separate male and female clothes and rule out cross-gender purchasing.

Black hairstyles

The grooming, cutting and styling of hair is an important cultural practice and symbolic activity for all young people. Hair has long been a medium of significant statements about self and society in which symbolic meanings are invested. Hairstyle has also been a central component in a variety of subcultural expressions: from the DA quiff of the teds to the long hair of the hippies to the crop of the skinheads.

Hairstyling practices amongst black British youth, however, are a particularly lively and creative field for particularized grounded aesthetics where young people are able to seize some degree of symbolic control in their everyday lives. Black hairstyles are popular art forms which articulate a variety of aesthetic solutions to some of the problems created by racism, for hair, along with skin colour, is one of the most visible signs of racial difference. Racism, historically, has devalued the material qualities of black people's hair, seeing it only in negative terms. Aesthetic presuppositions have long been closely intertwined with rationalizations of racial domination – aesthetics which stem from Western codes of beauty where whiteness epitomizes all that is good, true and beautiful.

In the 1960s black liberation movements proposed the slogan 'Black is beautiful' to contest the hegemony of this white aesthetics with a grounded aesthetics of its own. Fully aware that such hegemony depended on the subjective internalization of these norms and values, the Afro hairstyle was adopted by Afro-Americans as an outward affirmation of an empowering sense of Black Pride. In the Caribbean context, the popularization of Rastafarian beliefs served a similar purpose. Dreadlocks became emblematic of a newly discovered sense of self. After centuries of negation, such styles inverted the binary logic of white bias to celebrate the natural qualities of black hair.

Hair has thus been a key site of semantic struggle over the significance of racial difference, a struggle to negate the very categories of racial oppression itself. In Rastafari, for example, the open signification of dreadness, through the growing of locks, transposes the difference already immanent in the acceptable attribute of dark skin into open symbolic struggle, drawing attention to that least acceptable attribute of 'blackness' – woolly hair.

In the 1980s, however, these forms of cultural resistance drawing on a grounded aesthetic of naturalness and authenticity have been joined by another set of cultural strategies in the medium of hair. These turn around a grounded aesthetic of artifice that works in and against the codes of the dominant culture, through hybridity, syncretism and interculturation. Innovation occurs through appropriations of elements from the dominant culture, which are marked off and differentiated by a creolizing logic of symbolic work and stylization that rearticulates and reaccentuates the meaning of those elements.

In accordance with these strategies, the 1980s have seen a whole explosion of diversity and difference in hairstyles amongst black British youth, in tune with constantly evolving and more fluid forms of black British culture. The 1980s have seen a revival of earlier, processed black American hairstyles from the 1940s and '50s (such as the conk and the Do Rag) as well as contemporary styles like curly perms (hair treated by steaming, relaxing and straightening) and 'flat tops'.

Traditionally read as a sign of self-oppression or aspiring to white ideals, straightening and processed hairstyling techniques are increasingly seen as providing the materials for an open symbolic creativity rather than as inert signs of an inner self-image, or as a sign of alienation or unauthenticity. Straightening is merely one technique among others, and a means to a symbolic end. As one young woman pointed out: 'Just because you do your hair in a particular way doesn't alter your attitude as a black person – or it shouldn't anyway.'

What constitutes 'blackness' is itself subject to historical change and negotiation. As one young black man put it: 'The way we conceptualize Africa is based on myth, textual references. You know a lot of Caribbeans have not been to Africa.' There is no such thing as total originality. Sources of style are always already culturally formed, already in play. Nothing is totally new. Young black people may choose and shift between many different available hairstyles, drawing on diverse sources for symbolic resources and stylistic inspiration, such as books, magazines or museums, as well as particular black stars in music, fashion, film or sport. Thus people make reference to Grace Jones haircuts (flat top), or Egyptian-style shapes to a haircut. Such references are informed by knowledges which place black hair styles in a historical tradition, a tradition in which young black people consciously position themselves.

The grounded aesthetics of black hairstyling have their own terms and criteria of evaluation. Choosing what kind of style and cut involves important decisions, beginning from that of whether or not to cut one's hair. Dreadlocks, for example, are premissed on not cutting and involve long-term cycles of growth and cultivation. Cutting and the decisions which follow on involve choosing from a whole range of techniques and styles, as well as judgements of manageability and convenience, taste and suitability.

Black hairstyling also has its own distinct social relations. Many styles require co-operative and collaborative interaction. They involve skills exchanged between friends and family, and relations of mutuality and intimacy. Hairdressing, as one young black hairdresser comments, is also a site of ritualized communality: 'Salons play an important social part as well. People come in, they talk, they meet their friends – it's the atmosphere of the place.'

Hairdressing is also supported by its own economic infrastructure, with a substantial hairdressing industry. Large numbers of barber shops and salons now exist in the black community. Hairdressing is a model for ethnic business success stories. The largest Afro-Caribbean owned business in Britain is Dyke and Dyrden, a firm that imports and retails hair-care products to a market that is more or less exclusively black.

Making clothes

Sewing, altering and making clothes are common practices amongst young working-class women. Skills and knowledges are often developed in the home, sometimes handed down from one generation to another, or learnt more formally at school, college or work. June, a young mother of 22, who has been making clothes since she was 14, had originally taken up sewing for practical purposes to make a contribution to the household economy, making dresses for her mother and herself. But this soon expanded into making dresses for, and with, her friends, buying patterns and material from the rag market to experiment with:

> We just used to mess about with bits of material . . . and wrap 'em round our heads and sew this on, and sew a hood on things . . . And we'd buy patterns and make a skirt.

There are a significant minority of young people who sew and knit their own clothes for reasons that are partly to do with pleasure in their own symbolic work and creativity as well as financial. As one young woman pointed out:

> It saves you money . . . 'Cause I mean, there's times when I think, well, I like this, and it cost £50. When I can just go to Birmingham market, buy some material for about a pound a yard . . . and look just as good as what was in the shops. And I'm so happy.

There is a symbolic as well as practical pleasure and sense of fulfilment for young people in being able to use their own manual skills and resources to make their own clothes. Joan, for example, says that she specifically enjoys the material process of cutting up patterns: 'What I really love about it is getting material on the table and just start cutting. 'Cause I love cutting up the patterns and start stitching it.'

Making your own clothes enables you to have some control over what you wear. It means, above all, that you don't have just to follow fashion, you can make clothes that suit you personally and in which you feel more comfortable along the grooves of your own grounded aesthetics. June says that she makes her own clothes because she doesn't like what's on offer in the high-street shops:

> I can walk around the shops, and I'm trying things on, and I can actually give up and think 'This is stupid.' And the actual price as well, and I look at it . . . and how it's put together. I can look at something that's been put together, so . . . *badly!*, really, and they're asking such a high price for it. I could make better myself. Like there's certain clothes and certain styles of clothes that I can't easily buy in a shop. For one, they may have gone out of fashion, and it might be a style that I particularly like, that suits me, and I can't go and buy that from a normal shop.

Many young people are both driven and inspired to make their own clothes simply by the high price of clothes in the shops. As one young woman pointed out: 'I went to a shop to buy a mohair jumper and it was 60 quid, so I thought I could make that myself. I bought the wool for £11, and made one nearly identical.'

Since the late 1970s, the rise in youth unemployment has pushed many young people into self- and semi-employment in the clothes sector of the hidden economy. For some young people, clothes-making is as much a way of negotiating the boredom of the dole as it is a source of income. Bridgette, for example, who knits colourful fashionable jumpers, says that she started knitting because she 'couldn't afford to go out, on the dole, so I thought I'd do something constructive, learning to make my own clothes.'

Jumble sales and secondhand clothes

Large numbers of young people buy their clothes from secondhand or charity shops, like Oxfam and Barnardo's, or from street and rag markets. Today, more than ever before, young people are having to rely on rag markets and secondhand clothes stores for the creation of style. The 1980s have seen a revitalization of numerous urban street markets with young people forming a major part of their constituency.

Margaret is 19 and unemployed. She goes to jumble sales frequently:

> I thought, why am I going into shops and paying all this money, and saving so hard for a jumper, when I can get it in a second-hand shop. 'Cause if you look around, you can find a jumper that's really nice and you'll pay a couple of quid for it.

For Margaret, as for many young people, there is a specific pleasure in going to jumble sales with friends to rummage through second-hand clothes:

> We always buy things we can experiment with . . . All types of coats, jackets that we just cut off to the waist, and things like that. You can actually make something old and quite horrible into something quite nice by just a few nips and slits and turns, you know what I mean. So, it's like, I don't know, it's good fun . . . That's what it is more than anything, it's just good fun . . . going to jumble sales, like.

Buying secondhand clothes is clearly part of a whole active process of symbolic work and creativity to do with producing appearance. Margaret again:

> You can achieve a certain look, that would be difficult to achieve on such low money, and also difficult to achieve by walking in shops, because they're traditionally made for a size 10 or whatever. And yet, you can find a size-40-chest man's jacket and it gives you the look that you want, but you can't actually go into a shop and buy it . . . that certain look. But by turning the sleeves up, or by rolling them over, you can, you know . . . Like, you can get your dad's jacket out the wardrobe, and you know 'Oh, this is trendy.'

The availability of secondhand men's jackets, trousers, shirts and even shoes has radically transformed the way in which women now dress. Young women buying and adapting secondhand clothes have been at the forefront of some of the major transformations in the female fashion body over the last ten years.

The process began with punk, which helped break down some of the gender restrictions on young women's dress and on female participation in youth subcultures. The androgynous look of punk, particularly its spiky hair style, became part of a general popular feminist style in the late 1970s and early '80s. Since then, substantial numbers of young women have managed to deconstruct feminine styles through novel combinations of masculine and feminine clothing items (such as frilly birthday-party dresses, ribbons and flounces combined with heavyweight boots or Dr Marten shoes). More recently, baggy shirts have proved immensely popular as flexible items of female clothing. Men's raincoats too have been made fashionable amongst young women, picked up at jumble sales for as little as five pounds. The sleeves would be turned up to fit the length of female arms, simultaneously revealing a high quality striped silk lining.

From secondhand and men's clothes, young women have actively created their own unfixed, fluid and constantly shifting grounded aesthetics of feminine style.

Everyday life and symbolic creativity

Introduction

The aim of this chapter is to try to give a direct living picture of some of the symbolic work at play in the everyday activities of young people not associated with any specific cultural media or products. Crucially we aim to show something of the terms, strategies and symbolic work used by young people themselves to constitute and understand their own activities in common culture.

This chapter is based mainly on fieldwork conducted in Wolverhampton. Most of our respondents were in their late teens or early twenties, single and, generally speaking, in working-class occupations or from working-class backgrounds. A substantial number were British Asian or British Afro-Caribbean.

We contacted them and spoke to them in a variety of places, including youth clubs, colleges and mother and toddler groups. Sometimes young people were talked to singly, but mostly in groups of up to five. Initial interviews were structured, asking young people what they did from morning until night during the week and on Saturdays and Sundays. Interviews were taped, and the researcher listened to them afterwards, to generate questions for the next interview. Later interviews were less structured, allowing subjects to use their own terms and strategies to discuss their leisure activities.

Perhaps we risk an overly anthropological approach in this chapter in presenting some of the meanings of social practices themselves rather than focusing, as previous chapters do, on the specific uses of particular cultural commodities and cultural media. This is a worthwhile risk, however, in order to emphasize a perspective from which the whole book should be read: that the symbolic creativity of the young is based in their everyday informal life and infuses with meaning the entirety of the world as they see it.

Language is the most fundamental means of symbolic work and throughout this chapter (as in others) we use and quote the words that young people themselves use to express and explore their possibilities.

The biggest single dilemma in writing and editing this chapter has been whether, and if so how, to deal with the 'antisocial' activities of excess drinking and fighting. These things certainly involve large sections of youth, especially those from the white male working class. But they are also the focus for contempt and very widespread, often sensationalized, concern. Violence, particularly, has become the index and displaced image for many troubling questions concerning the quality, direction and meaning of 'life in our times'. We certainly do not wish to fan the flames of sensation. However, we have decided to include such activities because we are committed to following through our emphasis on presenting youth meanings both realistically and in their own terms. We cannot avert our gaze selectively and conveniently when trouble looms and miss out whole tracts of social symbolic landscape which actually constitute the terrain underfoot as well as, often, the effective horizon for many young people.

This does not mean that we applaud or support such activities. Apart from their intrinsic destructiveness, they also help to reproduce oppressive race, class and gender structures of feeling, attitude and practice. Nevertheless, common culture teaches us that more than one thing can be true of, or said about, a phenomenon. If we can find a thread of symbolic work and coherent human meaning and feeling even in brutalized conditions and through degrading materials, then our general argument is demonstrated *a fortiori* by this extreme and limited case. This thread of meaning will swell into streams and rivers through sympathetic materials and welcoming symbolic channels.

In part our purpose here is to get behind the tabloid headings, to get at real human contexts and meanings. It is ironic, for instance, that in the case of violence the physical fight on the stage boards or through the celluloid image is accepted as a legitimate climax to other kinds of symbolic fighting. It is taken as an understandable resolution to a tense chain of events connected together through the meanings of plot and situation. Yet our images and understandings of urban violence in real life are ridiculously truncated. We're transfixed by the notion, symbolically, of 'gratuity'. Fights are cut off from prior and surrounding symbolic meanings: from all that went before, from the narratives, contexts and meanings which place and make them, these things which for the participants often remove precisely their 'gratuity'.

To reverse the currently fashionable banalities about screen violence's leading to real violence, it is certainly possible to suggest that something of our very capacity to accept and interpret violence in dramatic contexts may well (invisibly) depend on our own informal knowledge concerning the informal dynamics of aggression. This includes understanding the difficulty of seeking appeasement with dignity, appreciating the seemingly irrevocable cast of some events, and accepting that there are moments when no words will do but 'actions speak louder than words'. Violence can have a symbolic as well as a physical part to play in social interaction and in complex human meanings. We aim to draw back a little the veil of public outrage to glimpse more neutrally some of the human meanings and processes behind the apparently 'inexplicable' and 'inhuman' face of violence.

Pub culture and drinking

Drinking in pubs is a central leisure activity, especially for white young men. Three-quarters of the 16–24 age group visit pubs, on average, nearly four times a week.[1] It is much less central for Afro-Caribbeans and for most young Asians.

Young people go to pubs for many reasons. One important reason is simply to escape boredom and often the restrictions of the parental home. As Steve says:

> If you stop in the house with your family, I just moan. I wish I was going out. Even if you go and tidy your room up, they have a go at you . . . So you've got to go out somewhere. I think if I had to stop in the house, they start getting on my nerves and I start getting on their nerves, after a while, like. You know, they have nothing to do so they start getting on to you . . . When you're in the house like . . . it's the same four walls all the time. So it's great to see somebody different, even if you're just sitting in the pub, you're looking at something.

If you are looking for somewhere to go, it's hardly surprising that it should be the pub. It is one of the most, if not the, central leisure institutions of white adult British culture. Young people turn towards it not only for 'something to do' but also as a way of identifying with adults, of becoming more adult and seeking acceptance by adults as an adult. The under-age thrill of successfully ordering alcohol in public, in 'The Public', is one of the markers of passing from childhood.

The pub is also an extremely social environment which announces immediately that here is a place which is about relaxation, leisure and pleasure – polar opposites to the formal qualities of work and school. The direct effect of alcohol relaxes the self and distances the real world, as does the warmth, size, comfort and protection of the pub. But the 'good pub' is one that concentrates many good things. As one of our male (employed) respondents says, 'Women, cheap beer, good beer, loud music'. The media shape young people's leisure activities throughout and the pub is no exception. Pubs are enjoyable partly because they allow young people to see and hear videos of the latest pop hits as well as classic 'evergreens'. They also allow access to expensive media and playback hardware beyond the reach of domestic finances.

> STEVE: There's one [a satellite dish to receive MTV, the music video television station] in a pub in Bilston, Bull's Head. You used to have to pay for a video in there, 50p for two sides. Now you just sit there and watch MTV . . . The in-thing is CDs, compact discs. You pay 50p for two sides on the CD. The thing is, it's off albums, not just the chart thing.
> NEIL: You get maybe on a juke box a hundred songs. On a compact disc you get 2,000. 'Cause they're only small. They're excellent. On a juke box like, it's singles. You know, the 45s, but on a compact disc, it's the album and you can have what track you want off each album like . . .

From the point of view of space, architecture, design, technology and devotion to pleasure pubs are much grander than the home. That is obviously part of their attraction. But this is not the end of the story. There are more illicit pleasures. For many young men the entry into the pub, especially on a Saturday night, is also the start or the promise of a kind of adventure, reflected symbolically in some of the more outlandish 'theme styling' of refurbished 'leisure pubs'. This adventure or promise is about the suspension of the given, the mundane and the everyday. It starts in the head and in the immediate social group with the physical effects of alcohol, but it produces changes there whose ripple can and does spread to make waves outside.

The social context of drinking operates to maximize consumption for many young men. There's no shame in it. It's done with others. Round-buying reflects and reinforces social and cultural solidarity. It is often a competitive activity. The amount consumed is related to how much of a 'man' you are, and the 'men' encourage each other in their 'manliness'.

> DEAN: When you're drinking, you always want to drink more than the other person. You always think you can take the most. If you go drinking, you're a man.

For young women, by contrast and to underline the case, drinking is not social, nor competitive, nor encouraged by the group. Excess consumption certainly emphasizes public gender identity but in ways which are felt to be negative, especially given the realities of dealing with a predatory and sexist environment:

> SANDRA: It's not feminine [to drink in excess]. My friend, she got drunk and I just left her there and then. 'Cause she was just slaggin' around. And I just, I just said, 'If you're gonna be like that, that's your problem.' And I just walked out. And I went home.

Being drunk produces uncertainty and, with it, potential danger. In particular, however unjustly and unfairly, it runs the risk of being perceived to be 'slagging around', immoderately displaying sexual availability.

For young men, however, there seems to be a positive welcoming of uncertainty and its possible dangers. It defeats boredom and seems to open up symbolic and real possibilities not available in normal life. They view drinking as that which sets up a situation, an atmosphere where anything might happen. The physiological effects of alcohol are interpreted to mean loss of control – an existential freeing of the self to an uncertainty which seems to be 'new' or 'different' every time. It opens the way to adventure whose possibility constitutes a kind of grounded aesthetics of risk and risk-taking. Risk is esteemed. The unexpected adventures which follow might be trivial: a bet, a 'piss-take', cheeking others or elders. They might be nothing at all except a frisson and heightened atmosphere of possibility with your mates in the pub. They might be serious, or escalate into it: setting out to gatecrash a party; being stopped by the police; getting into a fight; passing out in strange places. It's almost as if some young men want to invent, through drink, their own trials by performance in uncertain situations. The kinds of risks they take, the way they structure these risks, the way they deal with them, indicate, of course, components of young masculinity. Such components include improvisation, 'wit', 'guts', indifference to pain resulting from foolhardy actions, 'devil-may-care' irresponsibility.

> DAVID: When you've had a bit of drink, you'd do anything . . . you just feel wild more than anything.
> DEAN: You feel lucky as well.
> DAVID: No matter how big they are, you think, I'll have a go at him.
> ANDREW: Sometimes you go drinking and you go home, pissed

out of your brains, and the next day you think, 'Was it reality or a dream?'

DAVID: Some time ago me mum found me in the verandah, just lying flat. I must have passed out.

DEAN: I've jumped in the canal pissed and everything, off the bridge. You do all sorts of funny things, don't you?

ANDREW: You find it ever so funny when you do it. I mean, if somebody fell over, you'd laugh your head off.

DEAN: You wouldn't be able to stop laughing. Or someone would say, 'Go and do this.' And you'll go and do it.

ANDREW: You do mad things that you wouldn't dare.

The sense of release, adventure and possibility is partly about the symbolic creativity of overthrowing, ignoring or transcending conventions and normally approved patterns of behaviour and activity. These are seen often as, by definition, restrictive and boring. Many young people feel that they have no possibilities for 'safe adventures'. This may say as much about the conventional possibilities we provide as about the risky and antisocial ones they pursue.

Street survival: the dramatic permutations of 'hardness'

From the point of view of the vast majority of individual young men, it is not their own individual actions or potential actions which make large parts of the urban environment unsafe, threatening or violent. From their point of view it is already unsafe. This is quite independent of their own actions or non-actions. Far from their threatening it, the street threatens them. This is a given for many young men. For them only social theorists and do-gooders have the safety and luxury to worry about how it comes to be like that. The problem isn't to understand why or how urban violence comes about, still less to monitor your own contribution to it. The problem is simply how to survive it. And to survive it with some dignity and humanity. If we look closely here there are some terrible but surprising grounded aesthetics.

The fundamental issue for most young men in urban areas and locations where there hangs a fear of violence is *not* to fight as often as possible, but as little as possible. Most of all, the aim is to maintain honour and reputation whilst escaping intimidation and 'being picked on'. To achieve this you have to grapple with the complexities of 'hardness' in social performance:

JONATHAN: It's a sort of feeling of being known as a hard person. Like sort of going around and knowing that no one's gonna mess with you because you're hard . . . Being hard is all to do with how you put yourself across.

'Hardness' can be both an inner and an outer quality. It is also related directly to masculinity, its codes and public honours. There are several permutations of hardness with performance. All have their relation to masculine reputation.

> JONATHAN: How hard you act and how hard you are are two different things. Like there's some people who act really hard but they just aren't at all. Put down in one punch. Whereas other people keep themselves to themselves and you go up to them, you have a fight with them, and they take your punch, no trouble, and when they throw a punch at you, you know about it.
>
> ANDREW: You can be hard and act hard, and you can not act hard and be hard, or you can act hard and not be hard. I think the best of them is to be hard and not act hard . . .

The space between inner and outer meanings is worked through in what can be thought of as a dramatic grounded aesthetic: acting out your own performance and interpreting the public performances of others.

> STEVE: You got to watch people like, and see how they're acting. You can always tell when they're trying to act as if they're hard, you can always tell the quiet ones. They just stand there . . . The quiet ones nearly always turn out to be the hardest.

The worst of the permutations is to be somebody who acts hard but is not really hard 'inside'. Such a person creates an external persona that is unmatched by bodily force and skill. He is not what he appears to be. He is in danger because of this:

> STEVE: If you keep yourself to yourself, nothing will happen, but if you start going around acting hard or something, when you aren't, people are going to come down on you.

Someone who acts and is hard is preferable. At least the exterior is matched by inner qualities. But the most respected permutation is dissimulation, 'to be hard and not act hard'. This is to have substance, the 'right stuff', but not feel the need to display it:

> NEIL: A mate'll respect you if you walk away from drunkenness.
>
> STEVE: If anyone comes up to you and says 'Do you want a fight?' you say, 'Fuck off.' If they don't, you just beat them up. You give them a chance to walk away. Say 'I don't want to

fight, all right? I don't want no trouble, just go away like.'
You're still standing your ground, you're standing there
saying, 'Go away.'

The one who is provoked speaks before hitting. Respect is gained by
negotiating with an antagonist. This is part of 'standing your
ground' and is preferable to fighting. None of this works, however,
unless you are prepared to fight *in extremis*. The shadow and the
substance intertwine. The performance and the inner reality
overlap.

There is a tight moral and dramatic economy here. But it can
easily break down. External appearances are not a good guide to the
reality of danger. It is not easy to judge the line where giving
someone 'the chance to walk away' becomes undignified appeasement. It is not easy to maintain both dignity and safety. Symbolic
rather than physical management of tension is always preferred by
most and provides the norms for behaviour. But real fighting
remains the final arbitration. 'Hard-knocks' and 'nut-cases' who
seem to like fighting and who can offer unexpected open and
demeaning provocation have to be dealt with. For some reason they
don't know, or won't play, 'the game'.

More important, drink routinely complicates or destabilizes the
balance of the dramatic economy. Its buzz, frisson and grounded
aesthetics of risk enable the unexpected; 'one thing leads to
another', somebody feels 'lucky' or 'wild' so 'anything can happen'.
Drink makes unreasonable attack and foolhardy defence much
more likely. Were it not for 'hard-knocks' and drink, the menacing
aspects of urban social life might simply resolve into a series of
honourable stand-offs. But when the gauntlet is thrown down,
masculine honour seems to demand an answer. Aided by drink, the
drama becomes compulsive.

Andrew recounted the events surrounding a fight he'd been
involved in recently. He and his mate were drunk, his mate had
been beaten up, and those around him were then calling him a
'wanker' for not fighting single-handedly against the large group
that had beaten up his mate:

> ANDREW: Everyone was calling me a wanker . . . In a way I felt I
> had to do it [fight] to prove myself I was strong . . . To prove
> I wasn't scared of them. I mean, I was [scared] . . . I mean, I
> wouldn't do it if I was sober. I wouldn't go, 'Oh, fuck, let's go
> and get battered by twenty kids!' I'll just look harder . . . and
> they won't call me a wanker . . . When you're pissed, you go
> 'fuck', you can have your head split.

Andrew had to fight, not just to defend his mate, but, more importantly, his own honour and standing. Harsh, it seems unanswerable,
judgements and exclusions wait on failure:

> ANDREW: They'd just laugh and leave you out. Say, forget about
> you. 'He daren't hit back, so we may as well forget him
> now.'

Sometimes it's necessary to lose physically in order to win psychologically and socially.

Once embarked, however unwillingly, on a violent encounter,
there seems to arise another, darker, excitement that eclipses some
of the previous moral and social calculus. We can think of it as a
nihilistic grounded aesthetic – the incomprehensible buzz of the
momentary disappearance of all meaning. Courting this prospect
may lead a minority to provoke incidents deliberately, 'nutters' and
'hard-knocks' certainly, but also sometimes 'normal' kids who are
drunk, bored 'out of their minds', 'pissed off' about something, or
desperate to find energy and excitement from somewhere *that
night*. Those who've been involved in fights say that they feel
suddenly stronger, experience no pain and find the situation
strangely compelling.

> ANDREW: I've found that when I'm drunk, I'm stronger . . .
> When you're drunk as well, you don't feel the pain . . . You
> feel the force, but not the pain. It's a weird sensation, scary
> and good. People like to be scared, like on roller coasters . . .
> scary because it's different, you ain't used to it. That's why
> it's scary. But it's good 'cause you aren't feeling it. You can go
> back for longer.

This feeling of reckless strength is essential to any real prospect of
winning a fight. It is part of, tests and reproduces 'hardness', being
able to detonate an explosion of physicality in extreme situations.
Andrew again:

> It's just a waste of time having a fight if you don't feel hard.
> Then you know you're gonna lose, aren't you? I mean, you got
> to feel hard to think you've got a chance to win. You have to
> feel confidence.

Crucial to displacing finer feelings and fear with a robotic brutality
is the notion of 'losing your temper'. David and Andrew say that
they feel no pain in a fight because they 'get in a temper'. 'Losing
your temper' seems to be losing yourself as well, losing the humdrum of the everyday, momentarily, for an entirely different state of
being:

KEITH: You don't feeling nothing. When they're hitting you, you don't know.

ANDREW: You're so busy concentrating... You feel the hit, but you don't feel the pain. Pressure, but no pain.

DAVID: You'd just want to hit him and concentrate on hitting him. If someone just punched you without [you] being in a temper, it would hurt. If it was unexpected. But once you're in a temper, you just don't care. You don't give a toss.

JC: Is it exciting, then, when you're in a temper? ... You don't feel anything?

ANDREW: It's excitement, really, ain't it?

KEITH: Then it's all over, ain't it! [Laughs] It's over too quick. You don't realize what's happened and then, when you walk away, you say, 'Did I win? Or did I lose? Or what!'

Being in a fight seems to heighten your sense of reality by removing you from its conventions. The usual capacity to see events unfold is lost; there is no past, no future, only a very consuming present. This radical transformation of reality is 'exciting', yet ephemeral, gone as soon as it is experienced. Such intense and consuming absorption in the present makes it difficult to develop a narrative sequence to explain and place events, 'Who won, who lost, or what?'

There's an interesting connection to the media–violence debate here. For these young men it is not that violent media images fascinate because they lead to copycatting. It's more that, whilst their own experience gives a prior basis of interest, the media images add to this and shape it by giving it a grammar and more public language of representation. Media images fascinate because they can be used to name and to make comparisons. They can be used as symbolic material to make sense of that incoherent but exciting experience which in the heat of the conflict seems to be without its own meaningful signs and symbols. Media images can be used to try to make sense of how something can be exciting and incredibly scary at the same time, controlled from outside and numbing but also exhilarating – 'like a roller coaster'. TV images are used to try to convey the terrible fascination and as a way of trying, impossibly, to give a narrative back to the incomprehensible:

DAVID: It's like you're watching it and it's coming at you, but you can't feel it.

KEITH: It's like the telly, you can't feel the punches, but you're giving them out like.

DAVID: It's like someone's punching on the TV screen at you and you can't feel it.

JC: How's that like the telly?
KEITH: 'Cause you watch it and you don't get hurt.
ANDREW: You could give me shit and beat me with anything, sticks, the lot, and it's horrible, it, like, you aren't there, as though you're watching. It's like you see on the telly, it's scary, really. That's the scary part.
KEITH: You could've got killed then and wouldn't have known about it.
ANDREW: It ain't getting beat up that's scary, it's that you can't feel anything and you don't know what's happening.

Later from another discussion:

KEITH: They bust your nose, didn't they?
ANDREW: Yeah, bust me nose up.
KEITH: Right across your face, it was, wasn't it? Like Rocky.

It must now be recognized that violence is irredeemably part of our modern culture. For some young men fighting unleashes a seemingly uncontrolled and uncontrollable power. This power is admired and exciting, yet simultaneously dangerous and frightening. Both emotions are way beyond the range of middle-class and conventional notions of the importance of control at all times, except perhaps in the safe outer reaches of 'art for art's sake'. 'Hardness' has very wide currency and respect. It indicates the readiness, if necessary and under pressure, to risk the self and to try to control the dangerous and contradictory forces of violence.

Ironically the cultural system which limits and places this dangerous power is very much about control and performance: a *drama* of presenting and reading appearance and intention. To be lacking in control is very much looked down on. Control and power, very real physical and social stakes and the inherent risks and meanings of being outside the law make violence and its associated dramas potent symbolic materials to displace or disrupt given official and institutional meanings. These materials help in the construction and reconstruction of alternative ways of being in and seeing the world, of alternative values and ways of valuing people.

Some of these values may be repellent. They undoubtedly help to reproduce a certain kind of masculinity, as well as reproduce a dangerous acceptance of unacceptable violence. This has particular implications for women in the home where symbolic disputes can all too easily find a physical resolution. It can spread over as a threatening quality to the whole of our common cultural experience, making public space unsafe for all, but especially for women.

But these values and identities also concern a desperate kind of honour, a strange respect for the space around dignity and a mad courage which confronts banality with really live drama. Whether we like them or not, these are some of the contradictory living arts of survival – physical, psychic, cultural. Horrifyingly, hynotizingly, they contain some of their own specific grounded aesthetics. Outside condemnation, without understanding or alternative, shows up the limits of the observer as well as those of the observed. Alternatives to and ideas and plans for the safer resolutions of the compelling dramas of violence should be what exercise our imaginations.

'I'll be better next time around'

Sports and games provide materials, activities and social relationships which have symbolic as well as physical meanings and uses. They provide resources towards the symbolic work of cultural expression and formation of cultural identity. This may not always be planned for by the providers or conducted in the terms which they set out. It may not be so much about the ideal 'ungendered' improvement of health as a symbolic working through and creative testing of more profane everyday senses of what it is to be men and women in this society – but especially men. Whatever else may be said sports and games certainly involve symbolic creativities which must be recognized.

The quantitative importance of sport for young people is easily demonstrated from available statistics for the United Kingdom. While 54 per cent of all men and 35 per cent of all women participated in some sport activity in the prior four weeks, 66 per cent of young men and 43 per cent of young women between 16 and 19 years of age participated during the prior four weeks. The five sports most popular with young participants are walking (18 per cent), snooker/billiards/pool (17 per cent), darts (13 per cent), swimming (12 per cent) and football (10 per cent) (*General Household Survey*, 1983). These figures point to a high degree of interest in minority sports which is increasing at the expense of traditional sports.

Young people's level of participation in sport generally decreases when they leave school. Girls tend to give up sport from around the age of 13, while boys are more likely to continue into their early 20s. While this indicates a significant gender difference in sports participation, this difference has been narrowing during the past decade as women increasingly partake of indoor activities such as keep-fit and yoga. Ethnic differences in young people's sports

participation are difficult to determine as there is little documen-
tation on sports activities of ethnic minorities. Finally, there are
class differences in sports participation: semi- and unskilled
manual labourers are likely to participate least, while professional
and white-collar workers are likely to participate most (Greater
London and South-east Council for Sport and Recreation, 1982).

Sport, like other leisure activities, involves a growing cultural
industry. Over 370,000 people work in sport-related jobs. Sport-
related consumer expenditure totals £4.4 billion at 1985 prices. The
more popular expenditures include gambling, £1.16 billion;
clothing and footwear, £770m; sports goods, £690m; sports
participation, £530m (Henley Centre for Forecasting, 1986).

These are the bald figures. What is their symbolic content and
meaning for common culture? Perhaps most importantly sports
and games facilitate sociability of a wider and more networked kind
than the immediate 'neighbourliness' of the street. They multiply
many times over the possibility of meeting 'new people' but still on
some shared ground of mutual interest and trust; in many urban
and inner-city areas this is absolutely necessary when encroaching
on other 'territories'. Sport is a neutral flag. It gives an immediate
explanation of presence.

> ROBERT: We started up a football team, we went in a league
> which my mum helped us run. So I helped a lot doing that
> and that's how I really started to know people from off the
> other estate, 'cause we had asked them to come and play
> football for us. So they come training to get in the team and I
> got to know them better. There's a load of them, I'd get to
> know their friends and so I knew a new group of people. . . .

For young women sociability is also central to their enjoyment of
sport with perhaps a greater stress on social relations between team
mates rather than with other social groups. As Jane, who plays
netball, notes:

> We are just all together, we are one big family, like that . . . We
> go out at least once a month, or once every two months, or
> something like that, but we're always together, we're great
> friends, we've got each other to ring up . . . chatting over the
> phone, and things like that.

Sports and games then supply a set of controllable symbolic
resources and connections which radiate outwards socially, but
they also radiate inwardly, somatically. They provide ways of
thinking about, regulating and developing the body, and through

that a sense of self. 'The self' is therefore at an important kind of junction in sport, constructed somatically to one side and socially to the other. This is a complex articulation both of meaning and practice which provides a rich field for symbolic work and creativity and for the development of a bodily grounded aesthetic.

Jane takes a pride in her ability to make her own body move as she wants it to and for as long as she wants. Not everyone's body has these qualities, so it is a comparative pride and distinction too; a social as well as a bodily quality.

> JANE: I've been in that club now for five years and I enjoy it. It's a fast game, you've got to be energetic, you've got to be fit to play that game. If you're not fit and you're not energetic, don't bother playing netball. We train for four hours non-stop, train for two hours and play for two hours . . . I love netball because in a way it gets me fit, even though you get tired, you get fit . . .

The nature of bodily grounded aesthetics seems to be different between men and women. The qualities of fitness and control are important for many young women for the prospects of internal wholeness being 'naturally' reflected in external appearances and ambience. For young men it seems to be more that fitness and control are important to increasing *applied skill* over something external, to becoming more effective and better at a game.

> GURPRET: If you play a game, any sport, right, you think, okay . . . 'I'll be better next time around.' You try to upgrade yourself really from being at the bottom to as high as you can depending on how serious you want to play that game, so you're always trying to better yourself.

There is also, for young men a sharp distinction between serious competition where the self and perhaps masculinity are really tested, and 'messing about' where skills are still exercised and developed but in a non-threatening context. These are distinct bodily grounded aesthetics for, on the one hand, competitive purposes and, on the other, for expressive purposes. They have different ways of linking the body to the social through sport:

> GURPRET: Serious, right, it means you're out to win. No matter what happens, you go out to win . . . But if you're messing about, right, you go for the shots. Like, say some shots that would be impossible normally, like, you wouldn't do in serious cricket, you take the shots and go for chances and things like that (when you're messing about). You also

improve your skills, you can just try new tactics ... You
learn more when you're just practising and that, like messing
about.

Spectator sports, in contrast to participative sports, attract many
many more males than females. For example, while 32 per cent of
all UK males have gone to a football match in the past twelve
months, only 8 per cent of all females have gone (MORI, August
1988). This concurs with our fieldwork findings; (white) young men
were those who talked most about going to professional football
matches.

Though the movement and control of one's own body is not
important for the spectator, its sensuous and communicative presence within an immediate mass social spectacle is of the essence.
Spectator football combines drama with spectacle in a way which
actively involves the watcher. It also allows the individual to
transcend local neighbourhood differences and rivalries by absorption into grander and more epic rivalries, into public though still
grassroot traditions, into solidarity and traditional loyalties 'under
the same flag' – a grounded aesthetic of place and belonging.

STEVE: I don't like watching it [football] on the telly.
JC: Why?
STEVE: 'Cause there's no atmosphere. Like you get the atmos-
    phere at the match, 'cause there's thousands and thousands
    of people there, like. You can see their fans, you know, you
    have a contest with their fans, like ... I mean like Heath-
    town, Ashmore Park, they're all Wolverhampton. Like,
    when we were at the match, there's no, like, difference. It's
    all the same one, it's all Wolves and that's it ...
JC: Do you feel that the Wolves are your team?
STEVE: Yeah.
JC: How are they your team, like what do they do?
STEVE: I don't know, like ... Wolverhampton's where you
    come from like, it's where you were born, and everything, so
    you support Wolves, you support Wolverhampton ... Like
    I've always supported the Wolves, and that's it, like. My
    dad's supported the Wolves, and I've supported the Wolves.
    My son, like, I hope he supports the Wolves.

It is often overlooked that the excitement of spectacle in football
relies on strong symbolic communication – tumultuous and
powerful, collectively and selectively creative. Each fan carries on a
process of communication, mediated by their own grounded aesthetic of the spectacle, with the play, the game and the 'local

heroes' on the pitch. This is enhanced beyond measure by being in the crowd which swells his or her voice and presence to epic proportions. Stevie Bull who plays for Wolves was the leading goal scorer of all four leagues in the 88/9 season. This is Charlie, a Wolves fan, on his 'local hero'.

> CHARLIE: It's bloody great, wild, when Bully's charging down the wing, he looks up at the South Bank and there's a huge roar and you're shouting like mad. You know he's gonna do it. You know, he's communicating with the whole of the South Bank. And if he does it, if he puts it in the back of the onion net, he goes mad, we go mad, the whole crowd goes mad. It's wild! Then he goes like an aeroplane with his arms held out, sweeping and diving in front of the South Bank. Then he does a gambol, he's doin' it for the fans and they love it. That's why he's a local hero.

And this strange spectacular communication seems to work in practical as well as emotional ways. Eighty per cent of Stevie Bull's goals this season have been at home matches in front of the home 'South Bank' crowd. The communication is about action as well as symbols. Stevie Bull's goals are willed. The fans are playing too.

Football chants and songs also show a marked degree of collective symbolic creativity. Sung to the tunes of well-known classic pop songs, they arise it seems from nothing, build up and crescendo into mass choruses. No one knows who's made up the words! There are many current songs and chants at Molineux (Wolves' Football Ground). They change continuously. This one is sung to the tune of 'Lily the Pink'. It combines drinking, popular music and football, perhaps the triple alliance of one important form of male working-class culture.

> Have a drink a drink a drink
> To Stevie the King, the King, the King
> Saviour of the Wanderers
> Football T – E – A – M
>
> He's the greatest centre forward
> The World has ever seen.

In contrast to the excitement of mass spectatorship, 'fandom' can also be a very private thing, an intimate communication from the self to the self, but somehow with all the resonances of the spectacle supplied through its connecting grounded aesthetics. Bill is a strong fan. His bedroom is a private temple to the Wolves. It also has a whole social atmosphere. Mostly it's about helping to create his identity as belonging to Wolverhampton as an individual, as a father's son, and as a fan.

> STEVE: I mean, my bedroom, it's [painted] all gold and black . . . I've got a big flag on the one wall, big picture of the team on another. All newspaper clippings on the one, and a scarf hung up on the wardrobe. There's all things about them [the Wolves], there's a couple of T-shirts, like, that was when they were a really big club.

Table and electronic indoor games are not about personal bodily fitness, nor are they about spectacle or local identity. They do, however, especially involve a lot of male young people. They are growing in popularity and provide their own kind of resources towards symbolic work and creativity.

Video games 'get your adrenalin going' and also excite partly because they simulate real challenging situations. They produce the possibilities for a virtual grounded aesthetic.

> GURPRET: There's a new game out where you're actually, you feel like you're driving a car . . . you're sitting in a car, right, the car tilts from side to side, [depending] on the way you're steering. Because it's got a simulation of the road, right, with bumps and that, right, the car moves according to the bumps and that.

Learning new skills and enjoying being skilful is central to the enjoyment of games. Delroy, for example, now enjoys playing table football and pool because he can see he has learnt many skills by investing much time and money on improving his game:

> DELROY: Before, all I used to do was hit the ball anywhere, but now I know what I'm doing with the ball. It makes you feel better. At one stage I used to . . . spend about one pound or two pounds every day on the one football machine . . .
> JC: What makes football more fun than the other ones?
> DELROY: 'Cause I'm good at it, that's why. I'm all right at pool, but I'm better at football. I'd say if you're better than most people at football, it makes you want to play more and well, it makes you feel good, I suppose.

Delroy enjoys developing his technical skills so that he can beat formerly successful opponents. But there's also a complex interplay here between the social and the technical which mirrors that in sports. Partly this is simply enjoying the space for sociability which these games provide. But there are several social possibilities for playing a game depending on how the opponent is perceived.

DELROY: If the game's good and I play with someone that I know can beat me, I don't talk, but if I'm playing doubles now, right, and I know I'm going to beat the person, we just talk all the time, or we just take the mickey out of him, like try to aggravate him, stuff like that.

One-to-one competition between male equals is a serious affair. In part it's about the construction and reproduction of masculinity as dominance and competence. But this masculinity is creatively tested and constructed in and through dramatic grounded aesthetics: as master, pushing and taunting someone to the point where he gets upset, watching to see if he does so: as victim, responding with good-natured stoicism, controlling yourself and coming up with a witty rebuff or something that might pass as such. If you fail in this latter, you're likely to become the butt of repeated jokes.

Such potentially cruel banter and the competitive spirit surrounding games as well as their aura of masculinity and masculine domination seem to put most young women off participation at least in heterosexual situations.

SANDRA: I don't play any of the games because I don't think it's ladylike to play table football, you know what I mean . . . I can't see myself hitting the ball, you know, and playing pool. I can't see myself doing that. It's not me. I like certain things, but those kinds of things I just see men doing it, and I think it's just because it's for men, you know what I mean.

As this quote and much of our other material show, the physical basis of sports and games symbolism makes them eminently suitable for the – even if creative – reproduction of *conventional* gender identities and definitions. In the case of young men this encourages what verges on, and is sometimes really, anti-social behaviour. Still, the creativity should not be overlooked. Contradictions make and produce cultural life. They energize from the inside many of the grounded aesthetics of common culture. What we wish to show is the balance of contradictions too well-known and understood in their other halves.

Dead old-fashioned

The notion of 'romance' is thought to structure the lives of many young women and to regulate their relationships with young men. Certainly the infamous double standard and fear of being labelled 'a slag'[2] influenced the behaviour of the young women we spoke to.

However, for a good proportion the notions of 'romance' and 'courtly love' seemed distinctly outdated. Certainly not infallible guides to action, they were rather simply materials towards the symbolic work of understanding their own position and possibilities. Like so much else, they could be questioned, contextualized, tested. In part this was associated with a particular critical ability with respect to the media; the puncturing of the myth of romance was associated with the operation of grounded aesthetics concerned to read, place and select media stereotypes differentially.

There was certainly a clear sense of what constitutes romance, and one immediately identified through omnipresent media images:

> JC: What's romantic love?
>
> YVONNE: Walking in the park, buying flowers.
>
> HILARY: I think it's stupid, romantic love . . . 'Cause I think it's like pretend. Like romantic love is the kind of love that you see on the TV and love in real life is love what's real, you know . . . Romantic love will last a couple of years, but love's there for ever.
>
> JC: But don't you have an element of wanting that, of wanting someone to give you flowers, sweep you off your feet, and tell you he thinks the world of you?
>
> ANNA: Everyone's bound to dream of that, but it just isn't real life, is it?
>
> HILARY: It's what you see on the TV.
>
> ANNA: It's just adverts. Like the body spray, you know, Impulse. The man gives her flowers (when she's shopping just because she's wearing Impulse). And you don't see that down Bilston Market, if someone's wearing Impulse. I mean, I wear Impulse and I don't even get one pea chucked in my face!

In another discussion Katy says that it's 'nice' when a boy is 'jealous' – 'It makes you feel like you've got some hold over him.' Again she goes to the media for illustration and quotes two young men currently fighting over Jane in *Neighbours*, but is immediately interrupted:

> RACHEL: What's the use of fighting? It doesn't prove nothing . . .
>
> GAIL: It's like in the old days, like in the old books, like *Romeo and Juliet*, they're gonna fight over them . . . You read all the old stories in all the old books, so.

Rachel's and Gail's comments suggest that chivalry is not so much dead as dead old-fashioned. Tragic love stories found in 'old' books

evoke a way of developing relationships which seems far removed
from the lives of these young women. They get more usable ideas
from television shows, most notably English soap operas. While
American soaps exaggerate ideas about romance and relationships,
English soaps, in contrast, seem more realistic:

ANNA: It [American soaps] seems to be full of passion, they just
seem to jump into bed with everyone, don't they?
HILARY: . . . But like *EastEnders* and *Brookside*, you can't forget
about the world. Michelle [from *EastEnders*] had everything
happen that somebody has in a hundred years! She's had a
divorce in a year, she's had a baby at 16 . . .
JC: What kinds of images of love and romance do you get from
shows like *EastEnders* and *Brookside*?
HILARY: Don't get married! Don't have a family.

It's not that the puncturing of 'romance' brings a real sense of
equality to relations between the sexes. The more negative features
of 'romance' seem to linger. Young men are still the prime movers.
Bold advances from women are still out of the question. There is
much suffering in silence. Suffering is reflected and interpreted
immediately in the light of 'feminine' qualities of appearance and
personality.

RACHEL: Boys are bad though, when you fancy boys, oh they
love it, don't they?
GAIL: It goes to their heads, they think that they're really . . . if
you, you know, let them know you fancy them, they'll let
you hang on.
JC: So what do you do if you fancy a bloke?
RACHEL: There's not a whole lot you can do, is there? . . . You
can't stop fancyin' them, can you? Have you ever really
fancied somebody and know that they wouldn't go out with
you?
JC: Yeah.
RACHEL: It's terrible, isn't it? . . .
KATY: It makes you feel ugly, doesn't it? . . .
RACHEL: It makes you feel bad on the inside.
KATY: It makes you feel like you're an alien.
RACHEL: And when you see him, oh God, he's lovely!
GAIL: You can't keep your eyes off 'em!

The critical engagement with 'romance' seems less 'feminist' than
'realist'. The problems of the double standard may not be over-
thrown but they are negotiated using a tough and creative repertoire of actions and words. This repertoire is far from being drawn

wholly from or used in the manner of the 'respectable' end of gender images, behaviour and language:

> HILARY: Like what you got to do when you're going out with somebody, right, they always try it on with you . . . A bloke will go off with a slag, right, but when it's time to get married, they'll look for the quiet, well, not quiet, but decent girl . . . So when a bloke tries it on you, you kick him in the donkeys and tell him to get lost . . . When I was going with this bloke, right, he tried it on with me and I thumped him and everything. And after he said to me, 'Well, at least I know you're decent now', you know what I mean. So sometimes it's a test.

Marriage is seen as a goal, but not through rose-tinted glasses:

> JC: So do you think you'll ever get married?
> HILARY: I will, when I'm 28 . . . I'm gonna get married and have two children . . . I want them all girls.
> JC: Why all girls?
> HILARY: I don't like boys. They're so aggressive . . . I want it to be an equal relationship [with my husband]. Like he goes to work and I go to work, right. We won't have any kids for about a year, so we'll be able to build up a relationship more, right, and then we come back home and say, the housework, we'll do it together, . . . so it's equal . . . I want to be a breadwinner because if you're a breadwinner, right, you know, if you bring the money back to the home, you got more say what goes on in the house then. If you're just an ordinary housewife, the bloke seems to get more what he wants and I don't want that happening.

Hilary disapproves of, rather than accepts, male aggression. She also makes some key points that feminists have made; not only is having a job central to a woman's power in the home but, more critically, the housework must be divided between partners so that the woman alone does not end up with a double workload. Yet Hilary's comments are idealistic in their way. By stating that she will put off marriage for ten years Hilary, like many other young women, may be deferring rather than solving problems. Similarly, by claiming that she and her partner will build up their relationship for 'about a year' before they have children, she does not consider that after that time, one of them, she more likely than he, may have to give up a job, if not a career, in order to bear and raise children.

Despite these constraints, Hilary constructs present and future relationships in ways which do not empower her partner at her expense. She mobilizes her symbolic resources in ways which also introduce more of her identity into relationships. She sees where relationships are constraining and tries to anticipate how best to cope so that she can still assert herself. Symbolic work and creativity on received notions of 'romance' – holding, criticizing, qualifying – play a part in this.

Work and creativity

Leisure is the primary space in which young people mobilize and creatively work on and through a wide range of symbolic resources. Even though its loss or non-availability is a calamity, most of our working respondents did not rate their work very highly as a source of satisfaction and human involvement. Some of them, like 17-year-old Ian, who is a dustbin man, find that the best thing about work is the money and the hours. Work is just the huge gap in the middle of the 'good hours'.

JC: What do you like about work?

IAN: Money, finishing at half past four. The money is good for me, because I'm only 17 and it's [the work] easy done. Like we have an hour off for dinner and then we finish at about quarter to four and just go back to the depot, play pool until about twenty past four, clock out, and then I come home.

For others the problem is the 'bit in the middle' – boredom. And it can be a physical problem as well as a mental problem, characteristically contrasted with the healths and freedoms of leisure:

JOHN (an assistant caretaker): I get really bored at work, the time don't seem to pass. I'm full of aches and pains all day as well, I seem to get everything – but as soon as I go home I'm fine, hobbies, watching telly, everythin' . . . Boredom, that's the problem . . . the place is killin' me.

However, symbolic and social activity can be part of work tasks and can produce satisfactions. For a minority we found a sense of creativity in work. Eighteen-year-old Neil, for example, gets great satisfaction from the work that he does with disabled people. He enjoys it for several reasons. First and foremost, he enjoys helping them to expand their leisure activities, participating more in the world which able-bodied people primarily inhabit:

NEIL: Like George Garnett, he's a cerebral palsy, it took me six months to get him to go to a night club. It's always something he's wanted to do but, because of his shape and dis-

figurement, he didn't want to go because he thought that
people would look at him?

JC: Did they?

NEIL: Yes, well, but you know, you have to get the fact over to
him that, forget them, they don't mean a thing, you know,
what other people think is not important, you should enjoy
yourself and make the most out of your life . . .

JC: Have you succeeded?

NEIL: Well, I feel that I've succeeded there because I did change
people, not a great deal, but changed them enough for them
to enjoy themselves, and . . . it just makes you feel good
inside, you know, and it boosts your whole outlook on life,
just to see people like that enjoy themselves.

To be able to achieve his aims Neil must be able to put himself in
the position of and to understand how it might feel to be a disabled
person entering a room occupied by the able-bodied. He also must
be able to provide the disabled with tools that will help them get
beyond this feeling. Both of these tasks require a keen knowledge of
emotional life. In talking with them and coming to understand how
they live and understand their lives, he comes to understand the
human condition more fully through an emotive grounded aesthetic which most work allows no play for. He says that he would
like to work with other kinds of disabled people so that he can
gather together as diverse and full a picture of the human experience as possible:

NEIL: I'd like to work with disabled kids, young kids, nursery
kids. I want a wide scope of life, try and collect as much
information as possible, because that's what we're here for,
we're all brought down to collect information, like you're
collecting information now.

Young mothers

Many of our respondents were young mothers with two or more
children. These women note that they have hardly any time during
the day to themselves. They are too preoccupied with housework
and taking care of the children and perhaps husband or partner.

MARGARET: You don't have time to get bored. Because you've
got too much to do. If it ain't housework, it's looking after
the kids. If it ain't looking after the kids, it's looking after the
husband . . .

LESLEY: . . . There's not enough hours in a day. There isn't

> enough hours to do what you've got to do. You know you
> don't have time to get bored.
>
> JC: You're busy, are you enjoying it?
>
> MARGARET: It isn't that I don't enjoy it and I do enjoy it, it's got
> to be done. These [kids] have to be fed, and washed and
> dressed and everything else, and the house has to be cleaned
> up, so it's just a normal day, everyday thing. But if I wasn't in
> a routine, I'd be in a mess.

Clearly, creative expression and symbolic creativity are not upper-
most in these women's minds.

Housework and looking after children can be physically exhausting. Of the half-dozen young mothers in our discussion groups two
complained of being physically worn down.

> ELAINE: I'm on vitamins and iron. The doctor's told me I've got
> to start and take things easy. Everything's getting on top of
> me, but he says I'm run down, really under, and he wants to
> test me water for diabetics [sic] 'cause it's in the family. He
> says I'm showing some of the symptoms. Probably it's just a
> lack of sleep, tired.

Neither she nor most of the other married women in our discussion
groups had much help with household tasks from their husbands.
Even women with unemployed husbands got little help.

Yet all these women make some space for rest and relaxation to
be themselves for themselves – and symbolic materials play a part
in this. The television gives them the minimum means of escape.
Many have the television on all day. Like most viewers, they
combine watching the television with other activities. They glance
at and listen to it throughout the day. Only when programmes that
they like are on, do they try to sit down and watch them. As Elaine
notes again: 'It's on all day, it's always on all day. If there's summat
on I want to watch, I will sit down and watch it. But if there ain't
nothing, I won't bother.'

If these women's daytime viewing is sporadic and involves only
partial attention to what is going on, their nighttime viewing is
almost the opposite. Lesley, for example, notes that she likes to
watch the television by herself at night in a kind of grounded
aesthetic of solace.

> Because it's the only time I can watch, usually my husband
> goes out at about quarter to ten, so that . . . depending on what
> time he comes in, is my only time on my own that I can
> unwind. I can't go to bed unless I've watched TV and unwound
> . . . Last night I went upstairs after tea for an hour and a half, me

husband says, 'What were you doing?' I says, 'I was watching
telly in the bedroom just so I could be on me own.' I like to be
on me own and I just don't seem to get it.

The most liked programmes are soap operas and quizzes. Many
watch *Neighbours* and *Sons and Daughters*. Some of them, like
Elaine, enjoy game shows because of the 'Excitement, the money,
just getting involved in the quizzes and questions they ask, and
that, and guessing the answers before they say "um".' Television
shows like these invite them to participate, to put themselves in
the shoes of the participants.

Young mothers do not constitute a monolithic group. Although
most in our discussion groups were somewhat demoralized by the
constraints of motherhood and maintaining a house, this was not
true for all.

Susan, for instance, took precautions as soon as her son was born,
to prevent herself from feeling too enclosed by the new demands of
motherhood. She began playing netball:

> It's mainly since I had Neil that I wanted to do the sport, to get a
> bit back, to normal kind of things, I hadn't really bothered
> since I left school to do anything, really . . . Sometimes I feel
> like going out. With the netball, I think, 'There's a good break.'
> When I come home from netball, I feel, if I've gone out in a bad
> mood, I come back all right, like, so that's my main break at the
> moment and I enjoy it. I'd sooner go and play netball than sit in
> the pub drinking.

During her time out she is able to forget about her domestic
situation by getting immersed in different and outside social and
symbolic materials which then act back on her sense of identity to
make her feel 'normal'. Susan also engages in other activities both
in and outside the home. She and her unemployed husband Scott
bought a video machine which has given them a means of having
leisure in the home. They play video games, which enable Susan to
intertwine some symbolic creativities into the dry texture of daily
domestic chores. She has a way of escaping from routine. Susan also
reads books, knits and makes cakes for relatives. She is fairly happy
with her life.

The two structural features which distinguish Susan from the
others seem to be having an unemployed husband who helps her
with chores, and having only one child. These two features free
her from some of the constraints that weigh heavily on the other
women and open up possibilities for more creative symbolic work
and cultural satisfactions.

The young unemployed

The situation is also difficult but in different ways for unemployed young people. Whilst young mothers lack the time and energy for much leisure activity, unemployed young people lack the economic resources necessary for more than a minimal amount of leisure, leisure activities and the possibilities for symbolic lifting through grounded aesthetics which they provide.

A striking feature of unemployed groups in both Wolverhampton and Sunderland is that they live in an increasingly small world as cuts diminish their income and thereby make it more difficult for them to engage in the leisure activities that other people take for granted. They are cut off not only from work, but from access to usable symbolic resources and the creative activities associated with them.

> NEIL: You pay your rent, you pay your food, and you're left with one night out [a week], if that . . . I go out once a week, on a Saturday. Like this week, I'll go out to a pub and I'll go to a club after. Next week, I can just about scrape going to a pub.
>
> JC: So it's like, one week you'll have a really good night?
>
> NEIL: Right, and then next week it's really nothing . . .
>
> REBECCA: I like to go out a lot, so I spend 50 pence a night, and it's getting to the point where you can't spend 50 pence 'cause drinks are 55, something like that. So, I mean, you just don't bother drinking. If you live alone, like if you've got a flat, then you don't see anyone if you don't go out at night. So you gotta keep going out. There are people who are really isolated, 'cause they haven't got the money to go out and meet people.

Going out at night to the pub is, for many of these young people, the only break in their very solitary lives. Some of them, like Neil and Rebecca, go to their local youth club during the day just to break 'the monotony in the days'. Their homes do not seem to be places where they find comfort and solace. This is probably especially true for those who, like Rebecca, have their own flats and therefore spend the whole day alone, unless they go to the local youth club.

Pubs and clubs are not the only places that these young people visit infrequently, or with very slim purses. They find it difficult to engage in other leisure activities as well. For example, Neil used to attend football matches when he was working. Now, however, he hardly goes at all because he 'can't afford to go, four quid to get in now!'

Contrary to what many people might think, it is not the

unemployed who are the most violent, at pubs, clubs or foot-ball games. They can hardly afford to get into these places, never mind buy enough alcohol to reach the requisite state of intoxi-cation usually necessary to get into a fight.

Unemployed young people find that their severely limited financial resources make their lives very frustrating, and, worse, demoralizing. They seem to feel radically removed from even the possibility of a good life which bites particularly hard if they have children to look after. Some of the measures felt to be necessary to get a bit of the good life – especially those for whom you're respon-sible – are desperate. As Linda in Sunderland reports:

When you've been on the dole for as long as us, you just can't afford to go out and it drives you round the bend – day after day. Then the bairn's asking for money or toys or clothes and you can't give any of them to her and you feel terrible – you end up not eating so she'll be the same as other kids at school – not shabby looking. And we've only got one kid – I don't know how people with more kids manage – well, they don't manage, they just live – just survive. And you have to do things that other people wouldn't dream of doing. Last year in the winter – it was a bad winter – me and some other women used to go down the lines pinching coal . . . I couldn't afford to buy coal at £10 a week. So we used to wait till the pubs were out and we used to put hats and things to hide our hair, climb over a great big wall, climb into these dirty trucks getting coal . . . dragging it back across the lines on our hands and knees, getting it across this high wall and then humping it across home. We used to get back at two in the morning. We used to be rotten dirty from head to foot and because you had had no coal the day before, you had no hot water for a bath, so you had to start boiling kettles to get washed. That's the sort of thing you have to do if you're poor and on the dole. People shouldn't have to do things like that.

Nor do most of these young people believe that their lives will change for the better in the next few years. Many of those who went on training schemes found that they learnt very little. They thought that they were pointless, demoralizing and led to no work anyway:

DICK: I was supposed to be painting and decorating. I only ever seen the bloke twice. So I just give it up. A month and a half I was there . . . He was always away, it was bad. And there wasn't anybody else could teach us . . .

JC: How about you Bob? Have you been on a training scheme?
BOB: Yeah.
JC: What was it?
BOB: It was general maintenance, looking after things.
JC: Did you learn how to look after things?
BOB: More like destruction. Well, they say, like, go and build us a wall. But before we had to build it, we had to knock it down. They don't tell us nothing about that.
REBECCA: They got a training scheme, but they ain't got no work for you.

In an economy which is eliminating many of the old manual labour jobs that working-class young people formerly held, and with no economic resources of their own, many unemployed young people hold out little hope that things will change:

NEIL: I don't look into the future. I live day by day.

And Raf from Sunderland:

I don't think very far ahead. I don't think things are going to get any better. There'll only be full employment again if there's a war. It's technology that's done it, no doubt about that. So things are going to get worse and all you can do is go out and try to create something for yourself – that's all I can think of – and what can you create on this much money?

Despite this poverty and demoralization unemployed people do attempt to express, develop and make themselves through symbolic and social resources. In Sunderland Linda has become the chair of a housing co-op. Holding this post has brought her to perform well a number of tasks which she would have thought impossible for a person as 'thick' as she considered herself to be:

What I've learnt these last three years [as chair of the housing association] is amazing – part treasurer's job, how to do rents, how to organize repairs, chair meetings – and it's just great the things you can do if someone takes the time to help you to learn how to do them. I knew nothing when I first started, but the professional workers helped us and we went on courses. Being as thick as I am, I never thought I could do anything like this . . . But now I'm trusted with thousands and thousands of pounds and people tell me that I'm not thick – and you can learn by being told you're not thick, and that's good.

For others salvation comes from an overriding interest and symbolic creativity in a particular cultural form. Neil is totally involved in heavy-rock music. One kind, 'gothic rock', is:

NEIL: . . . slowed down punk, really, but it's more morbid. It's got a morbid side to it. Most of it's like about death. Some of it's about love, but mostly death, but they do politics as well.

JC: What kind of politics is it?

NEIL: It's South Africa and things like that . . . Whatever's happening now, they'll write a song about it. Like most of the groups we listen to, it's all politics, ain't it?

Neil also symbolically works on the image that goes with his preferred music. He saves his money to go to gothic-rock concerts. When he goes he creatively and materially fashions his appearance through a bodily grounded aesthetic:

But the gothics, like they wear make-up just to look more evil and morbid. It's black make-up. Like when I go to see some bands, I'll pale my face out, wear black eye-liner and black lipstick and put grey cheeks in so it looks like you've got a death look.

Only a minority of the unemployed are involved in symbolic work and creativity of a public or spectacular kind. Many young unemployed people have such aspirations but lack the context, possibility or, more importantly, cash. But symbolic work and creativity do not stop because you are depressed, demoralized and often alone indoors. Instead it seems to become part of a twilight domestic world of the imagination enlivened by grounded aesthetics of fantasy. The imagination refuses to give up, but moves in surprising and unlikely ways – often taking on the very forms of normality which most of us are bored with and seek to escape. But working boredoms can be part of a distant or lost world for the unemployed quite as remote and attractive as any imaginative land. The common themes of housebound day-dreaming were, 'Just having a house of your own'; 'Sitting there, typing all day'; 'I fantasize about having a girl-friend'; 'I fantasize about having someone to cook for.'

These prosaic themes of imagination and fantasy can manifest themselves in private action: 'I used to dance in front of the mirror, when I was about 16–17, I still do', or 'When I am in the kitchen cooking, I think I am like her on telly . . . "Now you put the eggs, stir around,"' or 'I move the furniture around in the kitchen and pretend it's a disco.'

The young unemployed work and rework their own imaginative 'cultural scripts' just as would any playwright or writer. They are painfully grounded in 'normality' rather than in radicalism or the transcendental. They certainly show the central *cultural* importance as well as material importance of access to a decent wage. Most importantly for us, however, they show the tenacity of human symbolic capacities fed by the phantoms of cultural media even in the desert. What would more resources and wider possibilities produce?

Notes

1 *General Household Survey*, 1983; P. Willis *et al.*, *The Youth Review*, Avebury, 1988.
2 See for instance, C. Griffin, *Typical Girls*, Routledge and Kegan Paul, 1985: and S. Lees, *Losing Out*, Century Hutchinson, 1980.

—6—
Common culture

We are all cultural producers in some way and of some kind in our everyday lives. It is still often denied or made invisible in many of our official attitudes and practices, in our formal lives and communications. But the necessary symbolic work and symbolic creativity of common culture are now all around us. This book is aimed in part at trying to close the reality gap in our perceptions and understandings, especially for 'youth questions' but also in general. It is certainly true that we can't know where common culture is leading us. It contains many contradictions. But at least our analyses should not be altogether behind the practical realities.

The strengthening, emerging, profane common culture is plural and decentred[1] but nevertheless marks a kind of historical watershed. There is now a whole social and cultural medium of interwebbing common meaning and identity-making which blunts, deflects, minces up or transforms outside or top-down communication. In particular, élite or 'official' culture has lost its dominance. It has certainly always been honeycombed with subterranean resistances and alternatives but now the very sense, or pretence, of a national 'whole culture' and of hierarchies of values, activities and places within it is breaking down.

The specific contribution of this book to understanding these profound changes has been to try to document the creative practices which are already there and developing in common culture. These creative practices produce their own *grounded* aesthetics – not 'aesthetics' in dead corpses; in 'things' to impress or refine, grade or exclude, corpses to be warmed up occasionally in performance. Élite and 'official' culture can no longer hope to colonize, dominate or contain everyday life because there is already something there which grows from its own resources – a meaning-making and ordinary cultural production now full of implications for the rest of society: for politics; for the economy, for education and our sense of ourselves and each other. For the grounded aesthetics documented in this book are not only a rebuke to formal 'aesthetics', they and many like them should also be understood as the basic 'ordinary' micro-mechanisms which are producing daily and in concrete contexts what we regard as 'general' social and cultural change, 'periodized' shifts and reformations of human identities. Grounded aesthetics also therefore, and so to speak in the other direction, rebuke those who see social and cultural change being produced simply as a result of macroeconomic, social or political forces and trends somehow producing and sustaining themselves, to be commented upon and analysed by the élite but with 'ordinary people' serving only as their bearers, the passive medium through which they work.

The coming dominance of common culture marks, if you like, a decisive stage of cultural modernization, to be sharply distinguished from 'modernism' or 'post-modernism' as descriptions of internal form or design, where the 'mass' has become properly and popularly culturally differentiated through the active and creative use of widely available cultural commodities and cultural media. This is perhaps the last and the most democratic of the modernizations under the general conditions of late modernization. Of course it is uncertain, highly uneven and without guarantees. Finding and holding an identity in common culture is a risky business with certainties to be found only in slipping back past even the collapsing traditional values into regressive fundamentalism, secular and religious. These too may increase, but they will mark, actually, the final emergence of common culture as the norm.

It will certainly seem heretical for many to find the main seeds for everyday cultural development in the commercial provision of cultural commodities rather than in the finer practices of art, politics or public institutions. But we must start from unpalatable truths or from no truths at all. The time for good lies is gone. We need worse truths, not better lies. The 'arts' are a dead letter for the majority of young people. Politics bore them. Institutions are too often associated with coercion or exclusion and seem, by and large, irrelevant to what really energizes them. 'Official culture' has hardly recognized informal everyday culture, still less has it provided usable materials for its dialectical development. Worse, the 'holiness' of 'art' has made the rest of life profane. Official arts interests should therefore be the last to complain of commercial profanity. At least the anarchic market has been the great leveller. If an almost feudal privilege and mountain of forbidding anachronism remain in official attitudes, policy and administration in a whole variety of fields, then so should the 'worst truths' of the market prevail to continue to provide usable resources for the majority. We try to understand and to work for the 'best side' of this trend.

One simple way of pursuing the 'best side' is to seek to give everyday culture back to its owners and let them develop it. Let them really control the conditions, production and consumption of their own symbolic resources! But there is no simple, or even complex, way to turn this aim into reality. The commercial links are inescapable and trenchant. All symbolic materials are supplied under determinant conditions – not from the voice of God. Like real resources, symbolic resources are lodged in their own historical patterns of power and logics of production which simple idealism will not overthrow. The restless dialectic of the free street, and expensive studio will continue. Nor can we rip out the benefits of commercialism from its costs, certainly not in the short-term. But the process of cultural generation, change and energization could be less mystified, more transparent and shifted more on to the terms of the mass of youth experience and creativity, releasing more of use to them from the spin-offs and complex synergies of culture and commerce, from the 'best side' of cultural commodities.

We should also recognize some profound consequences flowing from the very informality of the everyday cultures of the young. In the way that the informal rejects or hides from the formal, in the very certainty and solidity of how informal identities are formed there can be limits and refusals as well as enablements. Informality often provides accommodations to and reproductions of power. It is the medium of the production and reproduction of informal power and control over others and of prejudiced – racist, sexist – views of them. Informal cultures can mirror-image official exclusions and leave quite unattended the formal, public and material questions of democratization and of wider access to symbolic resources. There is no ultimate or epistemological value in the unofficial or the informal for their own sakes. They can construct their own divisions and oppositions in what should be all of a piece – the shared, common human reality of necessity in symbolic work and its creativities. The 'best side' of the informal therefore needs to be worked for too, recognizing the play of its symbolic work in more public ways; strengthening its conditions of consumption and production; encouraging informal forms to be less opaque and more legible to their own producers and thus open more to questions concerning power and the real control of symbolic and other resources.

Understanding cultural commodities

The cultural world is much more varied than the mass culture theorists ever dreamt of. Individuals and groups respond differently and creatively and with their own grounded aesthetics to a whole range of mass inputs, from music to style and fashion, from advertisements to film and TV. Each of our chapters has marked some balances and limits in the way these things are creatively taken up and used. But one thing is common and insistently presents itself through all our work: the centrality to common culture of the cultural media and commodities produced for the market. We have to conclude that, in general, the public sector cannot do better than the commercial sector in supplying attractive and usable symbolic resources. There is no point in hopeless competitions with the market, still less in desperate 'artistic' or 'educational' inoculations against it. The interest of marketeers in differentiating and meeting the 'needs' of different consumers faster and more precisely through ever more sophisticated analysis of market 'segments', 'niches', 'life styles' and 'life stages,' as well as 'post-Fordist' developments in 'flexible manufacturing' may well serve to supply – even if more by accident than purpose – a continually wider range of appropriate symbolic resources for the symbolic work and creativity which interest us.

At the same time, however, we should recognize that everyday symbolic work and creativity in concrete contexts still draw most fundamentally on everyday informal life, its inherited resources, practices and languages. The suggestion is not that commercial cultural forms do or should replace or displace these things. The grounded aesthetics of symbolic creativity are not anyway 'in' things, they are 'in' sensuous human activities of meaning-making. It is simply that cultural commodities enhance and greatly increase the informal possibilities of cultural creativity and are now inextricably tangled up with them. The point is to try to increase the range, complexity, elegance, self-consciousness and purposefulness of this involvement. This does entail, however, accepting what is and will be an anathema for many: the possibility of a cultural emancipation working, at least in part, through ordinary, hitherto, uncongenial economic mechanisms.

Though all commodities are cultural to some degree, and though cultural commodities are the products of industries like any others in most respects,[2] it may now be necessary to recognize some of the differences between specifically cultural commodities and other kinds of commodity. To start with, the materials which make them up are primarily symbolic in that the 'software' or 'design' elements clearly predominate over hardware or material elements. What we value in a Buddy Holly classic, for instance, is not the vinyl but the symbols and notes in sound. These symbolic elements rely absolutely for their human values and meanings on shared symbols in communicative codes. This implies some kind of acknowledged relationship between sender and receiver not found normally in the opacity (as in 'commodity fetishism') between producers and consumers. It also implies some mental work in consumption, rather than simple material consumption. Cultural commodities can often be used repeatedly without being 'consumed' – CDs and micros do not wear out. Most importantly perhaps, cultural commodities can function not only as consumables but also as factors of production for repeated and different kinds of symbolic work, creativity and the production of grounded aesthetics in informal cultural production. This informal cultural production may be many times more significant in terms of human meanings and human involvements of time, skill, effort and satisfaction than the original commercial production. So far the analysis of commodities in general has hinged mostly on the processes of production. We should certainly not overlook low pay and poor conditions in the production of cultural commodities and services. But it is vital now to develop an appreciation of the creative processes and practices of extended consumption. Crucially, we need to recognize that consumption of cultural commodities involves its own processes of production (symbolic work and creativity, grounded aesthetics) in a way that is not true for other commodities. In short, a pop song is not a steel ingot.[3] For cultural commodities our interest, policy intervention and concern may lie more in what happens after rather than during or before manufacture.

We are not suggesting a re-evaluation of commercial provision and cultural commodities because of any putative 'equivalence' or 'value' they bear in the high-arts sense. Certainly we have no prior commitment to the value of 'free markets'. Markets and especially concentrations of capital formed in their supply can block and distort as well as enable. Choices may be provided, but not choices over choices or over the conditions under which choices are made – the cultural agenda itself. Nevertheless commercial provision does provide a range of materials through which grounded aesthetics can operate. It is important culturally simply because of its inevitable entanglement with, and contradictory enhancement of, the informal and its symbolic work.

We do not say 'let the market rip'. Nor do we do equate the state and state provision with unfreedom and the market with freedom. We do not suggest the vacation of all critical spaces. Admiring, accepting, understanding market mechanisms cannot supply an adequate framework and philosophy for encompassing and understanding whole human processes and sensuous cultural activities. Informal cultural production itself reminds us that creative human capacities will always work a selective and critical dialectic with the products of the market – enlarged and enabled by them but always exploiting a gap between how things are supposed to be consumed and how they really are or might be used. In our own historically produced situation, the point should be not to displace or destroy but to try to tilt these processes more to the advantage of 'consumers'. Here is continuing scope for politics and for institutional intervention.

It is important to recognize that there is no such thing as a 'free market' or 'free markets'. Markets and certainly the 'free enterprise' organizations which supply them for profit are institutions in their own rights, conditioned in many important respects by contexts, structures and limits provided by multi-faceted aspects of the state and of state policy. Different parts of the state provide all kinds of hidden subsidies to the cultural market and its producers: zero VAT rating for printing; the provision of workers, skills and ideas through the education/training sector; the provision of that whole economic and social infrastructure which is the precondition for the running of any business large or small. The point should be to try to recognize these links more self-consciously and to recognize and use whatever effectivity they might offer for the furtherance of the cultural interests, especially of the young – widening their symbolic access but also allowing them greater control over cultural agendas themselves. This would lead us into many policy areas not so far designated as 'cultural'.

Made messages

The emergence or, more exactly, the recognition of common culture must enforce a changed view of how communications in general now operate in modern societies. It has become fashionable in post-modern debates[4] to claim that the connection between signs and what they signify has been broken, that symbols and symbolic communications do not connect with anything 'real', that 'realities' cannot be spoken about, that there is just a 'noise of signs'.

Certainly a classical notion of 'sending a message' within an organic community from A, the sender, to B, the receiver, has been disrupted. For many purposes this model now has to be reformulated as a communication from A to many countless Bs via C, the modern international communication and cultural media and the international advertising, marketing and consumption of cultural commodities. C has certainly changed the nature, if not quite broken, the possibility of many communications between A and B.

An example may help. Whereas the early history of British popular music was in some measure about youth communicating with youth, pop records made by young people for young people, the current industry is now reorganizing itself around the general international marketing of standardized products and the sale of music and other cultural commodities to the widest possible range of adults. This is indicated presently by the rapid sales decline of the single, by the emergence of 'formatted', 'golden' radio (and TV) focusing on rock 'oldies' and 'classics', by the sales push on compact discs and by the increasing percentage of musical revenue coming from sales to TV companies and advertisers rather than to the public direct. Two of the biggest ever musical contracts were signed recently. These were part of the latest bout of the so-called 'Cola Wars'. Competing adverts will feature the premiere performances of likely hit songs from Madonna (for Diet Pepsi, fee $10 million) and George Michael (for Diet Coke, fee $4 million).[5]

These developments, it is argued, have broken pop music's ability to communicate exclusively within an organic youth community. Moreover the huge commercial success of the 'pure' or 'creative' singer-songwriters such as Bob Dylan and later Bruce Springsteen who try to communicate 'authentically' is held to have destroyed their ability to communicate to the experiences or values of particular young people in particular places. They're just remote, synthetic 'mega-stars' selling standardized mass products. Many 'committed' stars are reputedly disillusioned with the progressive potentials of their music and of mass musical spectacles such as the Live-Aid concerts.[6]

But we would argue that, just because a classical and organic model of 'message sending' has been broken, does not mean that the possibility of messages – of meanings taken from materials – in general has been broken or that, most importantly, coherent meaning-making itself is impossible. It is simply that the connection between signs and what they signify is more complex, and in some ways more exciting. The hubris and the myopia which go before the fall into the post-modernist fallacy of the disappearance of all meanings comes from, again, a fetishism with cultural *things*, their production and meaning for and within themselves. Rather we need to pay attention to their sensuous uses in creative consumption – their role as symbolic resources at the beginning, not the end, of (informal) production processes. The fundamental point which this book speaks to on every page is that 'messages' are not now so much 'sent' and 'received' as *made* in reception, often as a result of, or at least appearing in the space made free and usable by the operation of grounded aesthetics. Not only that, but certain materials and their potentials for meaning construction into 'made messages' would never have been available in their own organic communities. But, once available there, they can produce massive creative resonations; think of, for instance, the common cultural transplant through rock and pop of American black experience to the British white working class. Once brought together, live-aid concert-goers construct their own meanings. They enjoy the events in a whole variety of common cultural ways unconnected with the sent 'serious' message. But these meanings are still connected to a human empathy with others and to the formation and use of grounded aesthetics. As the music chapter of this book shows, DIY music borrows quite eclectically and unashamedly from a very wide range to make its own sounds. It challenges the corporate rock world by freely pilfering its sounds. Even the most doctored forms of music are available for political use and local interpretation. Youth 'creative consumption into production' is endlessly innovative in the face of changing technological and market conditions. The international supply and market mediation of music do not break the possibility of meaning-making and communication. In context and as provision of a widened range of usable symbolic resources, they precisely enable 'made message' communication.

Of course, it may be objected that these are special or romanticized examples. But even one example shows the theoretical space for our argument. The point is to try to modify simple notions of organic communication without falling into equally simple post-modern assertions of cultural chaos. 'Sent message' communication is being replaced by 'made message' communication. Signs as signifiers no longer simply connect with what is signified in intentioned messages. But this produces actually a widened scope for communicative work. Taken together and modified through informal work and creativity, received signs can signify in new ways to find 'signifieds' of their own, almost turning back the one-way flow of communication to make 'the hearer speak'. What kind of arrogance was it anyway that made of cultural communication only the process of hearing the songs of others? What cultural crocodile tears to lament a breakdown in that. What's really being mourned is the loss of the one-way power of communication by the cultural élite. But only they should lament that. 'Made message' communication is a fundamentally democratic force as well as the fundamental building brick of common culture, as the grounded aesthetic is its fundamental micromechanism.

The point is not so much that the relation between the signifier and the signified has broken down as that their difference is disappearing. Either can be used as either now and this is part of the 'significance' of how grounded aesthetics function. What is signified can be used riotously to signify. The chain of communication, A–B, has been made more complex not only as in A–C–B, but as in A–C–B–C–B

$$A$$
$$D$$
$$E, etc.$$

The 'made' (not simply received) message at B is sent out again through reconstituted commodities (C again) as a self-communication, or as a communication back to the sender or as a still other communication to another party (D) or parties (E, etc.). The process is no longer a linear two-dimensional one since the meaning(s) and direction(s) of the message(s) may well change beyond B. It is simply hopeless to think that A can control this. Nor is this lack of control inherently negative.

President Reagan may have adopted Bruce Springsteen's 'Born in the USA' as an unofficial national anthem to complacency and dishonest unity, but the same song also functions in common culture for many as an anthem of opposition both in the USA and in British white working-class culture. We have to be more alive to the dialectics and grounded aesthetics of communicative and cultural possibility rather than alive only to spotting deviations from 'proper' or 'meant' meanings. We need cultural entrepreneurs, not cultural detectives.

'Made' messages are not private, even when made privately. They have a social content and a dialectical relation to surrounding structures and to social and cultural change. Making (not receiving) messages and meanings in your own context and from materials you have appropriated is, in essence, a form of education in the broadest sense.[7] It is the specifically developmental part of symbolic work and creativity, an education about the 'self' and its relation to the world and to others in it. Where everyday symbolic work differs from what is normally thought of as 'education' is that it 'culturally produces' from its own chosen symbolic resources. Psychologically at least, the informal symbolic workers of common cultures feel they really 'own' and can therefore manipulate their resources as materials and tools – unlike the books at school which are 'owned' by the teachers, unlike fine art paintings which are 'owned' by the curator or, still more remote, the 'properly' cultured behind heavy mahogany doors.

'Made messages' are also part of the active work of consumerism and its role in common culture. No consumer meanings are written on blank slates. No marketeer or advertiser can determine, though they may certainly seek to influence, the 'message-making' of our consumption. One important source and resource for this 'making', the 'aboutness' of symbolic work, derives from the historical and social backgrounds of 'consumers'. They are formed through their specific memberships of different class, gender, race, geographical and age groups. They exercise their own symbolic work, utilizing inherited cultural resources and predispositions as well as performing active work on the symbolic resources supplied by cultural commodities and media, in understanding the possibilities and limits of their social roots. They are formed by but also actively experience and explore their backgrounds.

The early history of marketing was precisely about separating consumer groups into socio-economic categories so that products could be aimed at them more exactly. Modern marketing, however, has moved on from delineating socio-economic groupings to exploring 'new' categories of life style, life stage, and shared denominations of interest and aspiration. This is a crucial move since it attempts to describe market segments not from an 'objective' point of view, but from the point of view of the consumer. Far from being the passive victim of commercialism's juggernaut, the consumer has progressively been recognized as having substantial and unpredictable decision-making power in the selection and use of cultural commodities. In the case of young people, marketeers have moved on from defining them as a social group with certain material interests (reflecting their place in the labour/family/ education structures), expressed, however opaquely, in consumer tastes and habits, to 'youth' defined as a market category. Such a change has registered most clearly in youth magazines. For instance the traditional concern in teenage girls' magazines with romance/boy friends is being replaced by a new emphasis on consumption for its own sake. Adulthood is now achieved, it seems, by spending money in a certain way rather than 'settling down' to a life of wedded bliss.[8]

However, just because young people are addressed as consumers and without prejudgement as to their class or background is no reason to assume that their consumption or aspirations to consume are without meaning with respect to their backgrounds or to their current positions and relationships. To the contrary, consumerism can aid common cultural explorations of and challenges to a whole

variety of received notions and expectations – whether they be
associated with membership of particular groups or arise from the
operation of powerful ideologies, controlling institutions or élite
cultural assumptions.

The enhanced challenge comes from the way consumerism
brings new meanings and possibilities into the potential of symbolic work. The actual promises of consumerism may be more apparent than real. Advertising, in particular, has enlarged 'surplus
consciousness' and 'surplus desire', human aspirations towards and
awareness of potential satisfactions that may never or can never be
realized. Unceasing waves of advertising seek endlessly to manipulate with dishonest images of desire. They are frequently seen as the
most pathological aspect of modern consumer culture. Certainly
advertising can be unsettling, disturbing and often irritating in its
apparent assumptions about what motivates and drives modern life
(not, of course to be believed, and contradicted by the symbolic
work and creativity of 'ordinary' consumers *in context*).

But consumerism also unsettles tradition and convention. It
melts tradition and unpicks convention. It provides open materials
for the questions and comparisons of 'made messages'. It may be the
very impossibility of satisfying what it seems to promise that
makes modern consumerism and advertising pose questions more
sharply. Consumer commodities no longer simply make and place.
They strike back, criticize and make conditional. They implicitly
and explicitly pose questions and propositions: 'It might be more
fun consuming than . . . being traditional, . . . being married, . . .
going to trade-union meetings, . . . being a housewife, . . . being
bored stiff of work, . . . dealing with social security, . . . going to
Labour Party meetings.' These are productive direct questions for
the symbolic work and creativity of informal cultures. They help to
demystify previous certainties and to destabilize common-sense
assumptions. Questions can also be aimed at that very market
system which produces the consumerism which produces the
questions. Raised aspirations generate raised energies to be used
against opacities, exclusions and blocks, whatever their nature and
from wherever they arise. 'Made message' questioning helps to
provide materials towards the symbolic work of understanding the
'subjective' dimensions and possibilities of 'objective' demo-
graphic, economic, structural and social change as well as, no
doubt, producing effects in behaviour which reinforce these
changes. Some young readers of girls' magazines may well decide
that the power of consumption offers more to them in the foresee-
able future than does motherhood or marriage. In this light, greater
access to a high-wage, increased labour-market opportunity for

women and an emphasis on equal opportunities are seen as desirable, not as abstract political or social imperatives, but as the grounds for direct and potential personal and sensual satisfactions. Such are the real motors of cultural change geared down exceedingly small, not imperiously beckoned from above by 'politics' or 'economics'.

'Message-making' and symbolic questioning of social change for its personal possibilities make the informal symbolic work and symbolic creativity of common culture a crucial site generally for responses to and the workings through of late modernization, of cultural modernization. In concrete situations and in concrete ways symbolic work and creativity respond to change: economic; social; structural; cultural. They eat away at traditional and received certainties. They produce the possibilities of oppositional independent or alternative symbolizations of the self. They allow the exploration of alternatives to the transitions into adulthood laid out by the new regulating youth agencies. They push the definitions of and partially change the stages and meanings of the old conventional transitions.[9]

In a variety of ways informal cultural production, symbolic work and creativity process the directly personal subjective meanings and possibilities of change. They do this in much more flexible human ways than are possible in rationalized, instrumental and bureaucratic communication. Even as 'the market' makes its profits, it supplies some of the materials for alternative or oppositional symbolic work. This is the remarkable, unstable and ever unfolding contradiction of capitalism supplying materials for its own critique.

Current notions of 'post-modernism'[10] seem singularly ill-equipped to catch these potentials of everyday cultural response and symbolic production in cultural modernization. Post-modernism has declared as defunct precisely those modernizing forces which continue to engulf and revolutionize modern ways of everyday life in ever heightened ways. It may make sense to speak of 'post-modernisms' in 'art' 'discourses' (fine art, architecture) where there is a body of modernist texts or artefacts to react against. There is no such body of thought or things to mediate – or to form through counter-reaction – the symbolic work and symbolic creativity of informal cultural production. These things have hardly been recognized themselves. They struggle still to find sufficient access to usable symbolic resources, never mind to react to any 'modernism' or 'post-modernism' within them. This is not to argue that certain features of cultural modernization may not correspond with elements of what is called 'post-modernism', but that such labels simply don't help outside the 'Art-History' world. They are static, inturned and relate in élite and exclusive ways to *things*, rather than to open processes and practices. They are positively misleading if they direct attention away from the way in which modernization is still sweeping through, and producing complex and creative responses in, ordinary lives and their cultural productions. Common culture is not (as 'post-modern' culture is held to be) chaotic or meaningless even if it is invisible or baffling to outside formal eyes. Its inherently democratic impulses, its variety and complexity, above all its social connectedness, show us much more than does the formal 'modernist' or 'post-modernist' élite debate about how 'ordinary' identities creatively and 'commonly' articulate with, and are developed through, the restless, dramatic and contradictory themes of modernization.

An understanding of common culture may also have relevance to the high-art debate. There's a controversy raging at the moment about the dangers of high art's being turned into a business and individual works of art into commodities.[11] Clearly the notion that artistic practice might be dragged into the philistine marketplace is bruising a few sensibilities. But informal cultural practices in the shadows of the high-art institutions have never had the luxury of enjoying subsidy in seeking and developing their own cultural expressions. If the argument is about the necessity of subsidy, then why not subsidy for informal cultural production too? More to the point, however, is that a more complex model is clearly needed for understanding high art as communication and as potential communication. The fundamental point is that the 'relations of production' (who pays and/or controls whom for doing what to what for whom) of art do not enforce an obedient reflection in their 'relations of consumption' (who understands what made available how in which places and relationships).[12] It is wholly limiting to assume that effects (in Audience) must mirror intentions (in Artist). In high art and in their embattled institutions mismatches are taken to indicate incompetency – in the artistry of the artist, in the sensibility or education of the receiver. It seems to be feared that, if intention is made commercial or lodged in commercial imperatives, then so must all the meanings that are produced be circumscribed by market meanings. But informal cultural production shows us that mismatches between what is intended and what is taken are not only commonplace and inevitable, they are also important sources of creativity for informal symbolic work and symbolic creativity. The point for those involved in the high arts might be to abandon their self-conscious purity and seek to make the symbolic resources of high art as open as possible and at as many sites as possible for the unprefigurable work of symbolic creativity and production. There are many roads to this Rome.

Proto-communities

'Made messages' and grounded aesthetics operating under the conditions of late modernization provide grounds for new, emergent or potential communication communities – let us say 'proto-communities' – which are as yet unrecognizable, misrecognized, or only partly recognized.

Organic communication, where communities communicate within themselves and then outwards, sending messages about their conflicts, oppressions and material conditions of existence, is breaking down. 'Community walls' now zigzag wildly around the urban mass. Immediate next-door neighbours may know nothing about each other's work, workplaces or wider kinships. Often they share only their postcodes. Organic communities and organic communications are slowly disappearing.

Emergent and fissiparous proto-communities are and will be different in kind from organic communities. They are flatter and much more resistant to top-down communications of all kinds. They have different origins and different stakes in communication. They start and form not from intentioned purposes, political or other, but from contingency, from fun, from shared desires, from decentred overlaps, from accidents. They form from and out of the unplanned and unorganized precipitations and spontaneous patterns of shared symbolic work and creativity.

Proto-communities may sometimes have organic features in that they involve, for instance, direct communication around a 'consuming interest' (listening, dancing, talking) in certain types of music or in a variety of forms of producing music. They may arise in eclectic combinations of consumers who discover, incidentally, that they share a taste or interest as they meet in friendship, neighbourhood, school or workplace groups.

Proto-communities may often be 'serial'. These are social groupings not connected through direct communication but through shared styles, fashions, interests, empathies, positions and passions – sometimes shared simultaneously 'off-air' through the communication media. Metaphorically, a 'serial community' is a spaced-out queue of people rather than a talking circle. The same person, or bits of them, may simultaneously be in several such 'queues'. But they are still placed more than randomly or chaotically in social and material place and time and can, therefore, sometimes make or be made a living circle of communication.

They spot each other as more than strangers when time and place coincide. Connected proto-communities may arise in one-off celebrations of the sensuousness of, and sheer fun possible in, solidarity and collectively at mass events such as Live-Aid and Comic Relief. Though proto-communities have their 'causes' which bring them to life, this is not the same as commitment to 'a cause'. They make their 'messages', not receive them.

These insubstantial, shifting, combining and recombining communities may well share specific collective 'interests' and increasingly supply some of the preconditions for both the 'old' and the 'new' politics. There are many continuities in various types of proto-community with traditional collective interests, but such interests are uncovered through encounters with different difficulties or aspects of contradiction. Proto-communities connect with traditional concerns in special, private, ways – in the sense of alerting and developing individuals, through shaping identities and predispositions in 'made', not 'sent', symbolic forms. The development and emergence of proto-communities may signal not so much a fundamental change in the orderings of power, class and economic interests as a shift in how these things become lived and perceived – through how they both organize the possibilities for, but also frequently block the full development of, symbolic work and creativity. Collectivity may be working increasingly through 'subjective' factors – shared cultural interests and aspirations, shared interests in removing blocks to them, shared interests in increasing control over cultural materials and conditions – rather than through given 'objective' factors such as factory and neighbourhood's bringing people together.

This discussion of proto-communities might seem abstract and implausible. But the signs are all around us. They need rereading. Reality is in advance of our imaginations. Proto-communities, or aspects of them, have lain behind or helped in the development of much of the 'new politics' – feminism, anti-racism and especially grass-roots 'greenism'.

Although they deal with commodities in general rather than with cultural commodities and their consumption, many of the consumer movements are of particular interest for us. 'Consumer power' can sometimes be stunning in its effects, e.g. the recent egg-purchase boycott or the influence of Ralph Nader on the development of the American car industry. More widely, it's of great interest that the African National Congress predicts that their impact on South African politics in coming years will be more through black consumer power than through industrial power. In its own way the rise of 'consumer terrorism', as in the recent baby-food contamination scare and extortion incidents, shows some new and unexpected levers of power in the field of consumption. As commercial corporations spread their influence and power beyond national boundaries and seek to ignore or manipulate national organizations and even governments, e.g. the cancelled Ford Dundee plant after inter-union 'bickering', and the current undignified European scramble for Japanese investment after the Toyota announcement, it may even be that organized consumer groups will have more power over multi-nationals than do nation states.

Consumer power has not yet been recognized or organized in relation to the consumption of symbolic meanings and struggles over the uses of cultural commodities and the cultural media – if you like, a struggle over their semiotic safety and uses, and over the conditions and meanings of their creative consumption. And yet the signs of this are all around us too.

Consider, for instance, the aftermath of and popular responses to the tragedy at Hillsborough where 95 Liverpool fans were crushed to death. Read in a particular way these events clearly exemplify key themes of our analysis of proto-communities.

First of all, there is clear evidence here of the absolute centrality of 'leisure' pursuits to personal identity and collective meanings. More passion and energy, intensity and ritualism were poured out over these tragic events than over any recent industrial dispute or issue – with, perhaps, the exception of the miners' strike: 1,300,000 people visited Anfield in the week after the tragedy and the pitch, flooded over with flowers, was turned into a kind of sacred monument.

Furthermore we saw here a truly remarkable turning of the tide of communication and signification, not rolling into passive communities, but turned back to signify to the outside world. Football is often quoted now as the test case for how older, organic community sports and leisure pursuits have been broken up and decontextualized into remote spectacles by the cultural media, commercialism and commoditization.

Yet in this disaster it was precisely the cultural media and commercially mediated popular cultural symbols which were taken up, turned back and used by 'ordinary people' to signify *their* grief and passion. The media were not speaking 'for' or 'to' them, but were used to speak their own grief and anger. Fans spilling out from the killing terraces went straight to the famous players – the 'remote star figures' – to get the fastest human understanding and reaction. They sought out the TV cameras to show their still whole tickets as unspoken denunciations of police incompetency. Wide press coverage recounted how U2's 'With you, without you' was played at a young fan's funeral – in a chilling premonition she had asked her parents, only a few days before, that this music should be played at her funeral, should she die. 'You'll never walk alone' rang out across the nation broadcast live from the memorial service. For just a moment, hallowed traditional ritual and venerable national institutions were made to operate in reverse, themselves colonized by the insignia and passions of football.

More locally, as the fans closed in for mutual support and protection in Liverpool, they defied or contested insulting and sterotypical media images in an avalanche of the highest ever recorded complaints to the Press Council and in a widespread and still continuing boycott of the *Sun* and *Mirror*. A newly formed or reformed sensuous community around football showed its continuities and solidarities with local working-class community pride in Liverpool.

There are also wider, more varied and more invisible struggles and practices which confirm the importance of cultural aspirations and the enormous real and potential energies of proto-communities. Youth unemployment, low wage rates and insecurity have ravaged the economic and cultural possibilities for many young people. There has been relatively little self-organized protest and organization. Yet where the young have self-organized, it has rarely been around economic issues *per se*, but around cultural issues. This is partly, no doubt, because economic determinants and factors lie out of reach. But equally we should not underestimate that a cultural dynamic of organization and protest draws from an enormous reservoir of informal passion and energy and a sensuous hunger for access to and control of usable symbolic materials, their means of production and reproduction, as well as cultural assets and spaces necessary for their exercise. These things matter to the sustenance of grounded aesthetics and the formation of identity.

There are many examples if you dig. The current Acid House music and warehouse party movements show the disruptive power of young people demanding control over their own cultural space and activities. There are currently highly imaginative 'venue campaigns' being conducted in Norwich, spontaneously organized groups of young people campaigning for music performance and cultural centres to be designed and controlled by them. The Waterside project in Norwich now has premises and a budget running into hundreds of thousands of pounds. A similar successful campaign was organized in Telford, resulting in the Culture Centre. In the early 1980s, a group of Rastafarians sat outside the Council

Chamber in Wolverhampton, refusing to move until the Council Leader came to talk to them. Finally he did just that and promised them funds for their own centre which subsequently became the base for the Wolverhampton Rastafarian Progressive Association organizing its own sounds systems, work-shops and education classes.

In very inhospitable soil proto-communities struggle all around us to grow into sensuous communities.

Implications

What are the implications of accepting that we are all cultural producers? What are the implications of recognizing common culture, of recognizing the crucial role of grounded aesthetics, 'made messages' and proto-communities in ordinary people's lives? What lies beyond common culture?

We cannot be at all specific, not least because we don't yet know. But we do know enough already to suggest that a number of élite debates and complacent areas of assumption and practice are going to be thoroughly shaken up and changed forever.

The traditional and élite sources of cultural meaning and identity are declining fast and becoming broken up. The meaning of paid work, for instance, is changing fast, though there is and will be vigorous counter-attack by a variety of employer and state agencies. For many work has no real intrinsic value except as a means to livelihood and especially to leisure, to the work and symbolic creativities of its play. Some leisure meanings and practices may, however, return *informally* to work situations and link with and help to shape its informal culture, to the further chagrin of many employers. The crucial lesson for us to draw here is that we need a different view of human beings. If not, the young will soon hit us over the head with one. The contradictions are nicely bubbling now in the gap between cultural richness and possibility on one side and no work or boring work and lack of cash on the other. Soon they will explode (or implode) and become major issues in public consciousness, just as green issues have suddenly arrived 'from nowhere'. Rather than see humans as lumps of 'labour power', meaningful only in work or altogether 'redundant', we will then need to see them as full creative *citizens*, full of their own sensuous symbolic capacities and activities and taking a hand in the construction of their own identities. A notion of the ordinary cultural practices, symbolic creativity and its grounded aesthetics, associated with such humans will make redundant a notion of cultural practice as 'culturedness', criticism and appreciation. Understanding the processes and practices of informal cultural production will force us to see that there is a dialectic between consumption and production. Both are on a creative continuum, not broken between 'passive' and 'active'. Expanded consumption would produce new kinds of, and possibilities for, cultural production and new cultural demands in general – some small part of which might result in successful entrepreneurial commercial forms. All are cultural consumers before they are cultural producers. It is increasingly as consumers that we must first address them.

Symbolic creativity, especially amongst the young, remains fettered still by the lack of access to the widest possible ranges of usable symbolic resources and proper conditions for their use. Often the grounded aesthetics of the young are suppressed or even criminalized rather than developed. There is a clear case for supplementing the market with initiatives and free and open institutions directly to increase the possibilities for consumption of cultural commodities, including the self-directed use of electronic hardware and the new screen-based technologies as factors in informal cultural production, for those without cash power on the cultural market. Why shouldn't there be some kind of tax on 'cash' cultural consumption to subsidize 'non-cash' consumption? This may become increasingly important for young people over the next decade as the 'youth market' collapses[13] and products and services are restyled or introduced and marketed to rising market groups: young family groups among 25- to 44-year-olds, as well as 'empty-nester' groups among 45-to-59-year-olds.

Common culture will or should also change our sense of politics. It is absolutely not a question of touching proto-communities with the wand of politics, with a *political message*, to make them go 'public'. Those interested in 'sending messages' through a modern cultural milieu might, perhaps, more usefully spend their time and energy precisely in attending to the modest problems and potentials of collective sense-making in proto-communities rather than on the increasingly hopeless and promethean tasks of direct communication. Proto-communities produce, or have the capacity to produce from within themselves ('made messages', 'grounded aesthetics') moral and ethical feelings and capacities to fill the moral vacuum left by the market and to place against the unacceptable élitism and authoritarianism of party and institution. These capacities include a capacity for abstract judgement and for making patterns out of apparent irregularities; an appreciation of the social context and connectedness of private identity and of the shaping of private powers; a capacity to ask how any symbolic production affects the same freedoms and capacities in others; a consciousness in and of common culture as an area of choice and control. The possibility of connecting with these, and interconnecting them is the promise of the politics of the future.

The field of education is likely to come under even more intense pressure. It will be further marginalized in most people's experience by common culture. In so far as educational practices are still predicated on traditional liberal humanist lines and on the assumed superiority of high art, they will become almost totally irrelevant to the real energies and interests of most young people and no part of their identity formation. Common culture will, increasingly, undertake, in its own ways, the roles that education has vacated.

In so far as education/training becomes ever more subordinated to technical instrumentalism and to the 'needs' of industry, it will be seen as a necessary evil to be tolerated in order to obtain access to the wage in order to obtain access to leisure and consumption and their cultural energies. Of course, the development of science and technology is important (and full of satisfactions, perhaps, for the 'experts' and even for the new ranks of technical workers) as is effectively linking human capacities to the necessities of material production. But for the majority these things will never be accepted as the whole of life, as exhausting all the possibilities of the mind, imagination and sensuous body. Common culture is shouting this at us if nothing else; necessary *symbolic* work (i.e. cultural production as well as material production) has to be done too, and now increasingly necessarily outside or even against the exigencies of paid work and of the application of science, technology and training to work.

Just because the international tide of 'new realism' in education/training correctly perceived and exploited most young people's boredom with and frequent resistance to liberal humanist and traditional approaches is no reason for us to agree that *everything* which is not technical or work oriented should be jettisoned. This is a most alarming jump back through a hundred years of educational reform, a jump which goes in the very *opposite* direction to the movement of common culture, so ensuring, ironically, the further marginalization of even vocational schooling experiences to 'real life', or what most pupils regard as such.

We need an altogether new approach in education. Let us give the devil of work what is due, let us pay necessary homage to the goddess of technology, but then why not use the rest of humanity's currency for the widest possible imaginative exchanges and sensuous purposes. Education/training should re-enter the broader plains of culture and the possibilities there for the *full* development of human capacities and abilities, this time led not by élite culture, but by common culture.

Such a new project may include the study of some topics and contents drawn from common culture. Certainly applied training programmes (especially for the cultural industries), such as YTS, might start from young people's own enthusiasms rather than from nineteenth-century manual skills, connecting their own immediate cultural needs with their own everyday symbolic capacities. But more important than taking over its contents would be the necessity of a pervasive acceptance, understanding and development of common culture practices and processes: more informal and decentred democratic forms; symbolic creativity; the functioning of grounded aesthetics and 'made messages'. By the same token, the suggestion is not to junk 'high art' and the 'western cultural heritage' but to approach their contents, as the historical resources and traces of previous symbolic creativities, through irreverent common cultural mechanisms. If they or part of them can earn – not assume – their place in the tasks of the necessary symbolic work of common culture, then they will regain and refind their relevance. If not, no tears need be shed nor other attempts be given up to apply common cultural mechanisms. The material of common culture is always changing and could change in many unexpected ways. The high-art horror of the popular is misplaced and regressive because it looks at things, not practices. Common cultural practices, democratically understood and developed along their own grains, could certainly lead back to and creatively mine the symbolic materials of the past, just as they do those of the present. The democratic mastery of symbolic materials is being made a common thing, especially in the work of play – no matter what the imperatives, the materials, the media, the forms. Education becomes less relevant to this every day, whereas it *should be* in the vanguard of how we can proceed fully to take control, to live and master *all* of our present and past cultural experience. Incidentally, this would also be the best route, the future-oriented route, to the creation of a 'high-quality' workforce (and to their rational, human and necessary use) and to an entrepreneural opening up of new industries, though the direct purpose would be to produce fully developed cultural citizens.

What of common culture and the traditional arts institutions?

The traditional institutions, art galleries, museums, subsidized theatre, etc., can and should have a role to play in the development of common culture by opening up access to the widest possible ranges of symbolic materials without prior specification as to use or value. But this may mean equalizing not institutional access but institutions themselves. It may mean exploring new 'flatter' and more democratic organizational possibilities. The point of subsidy would be to maintain or widen access to the widest possible range of symbolic resources in general, not, in effect, to lessen access through intentioned and unintentioned forms of ranking. So far, implicit and explicit hierarchies of taste and value continue to produce formal institutions which include some but exclude and alienate many more. Simply put, the high arts need to be more available, in their practical conditions of material, social and psychological access, to informality and to the creative informal meanings of symbolic work. The real survival of any art form is in its being pulled – not pushed – into everyday forms of informal symbolic work and meaning, as these forms reach out from their own vitality, from their own internal life, for relevant and usable symbolic material. This is everyday cultural production 'out-reaching' the 'arts', not vice-versa! The success of Centreprise and Strongwords show that, in certain situations, traditional forms can be chosen by non-élite groups to express direct and powerful informal symbolic meanings. The recent successes of new initia-tives and explorations in some museums and art galleries in attract-ing somewhat higher attendances and the continuing success of many libraries in providing a wider range of symbolic materials rest, not on extending an old idea to 'new' people, but in allowing 'new' people and their informal meanings and communications to colonize them, the institutions. Clearer and more focused thinking could reinforce and greatly extend some of these already visible tendencies. The point of 'official' institutions should be not to order or value but simply to preserve – for democratic, unprefigured use – symbolic materials and fine or valuable historical resources which might be lost or otherwise not available.

It is too soon to know what they might be, but we should always be alive to the possibility of promoting, or vigorously supporting when they appear, new kinds of voluntary institutions and organ-izations developing out of proto-communities and utilizing their symbolic creativity. Such new institutions might reflect, perhaps, in the field of the creative uses of cultural commodities and the cultural media, the ways in which green politics and organization have risen so spectacularly out of general consumer experience. We need ways of developing proto-communities from within their own processes, from 'made messages', symbolic questionings and cre-ative responses to late modernization. Such means of development must be democratic, open and supplied without prejudgements – except, perhaps, for simple guidelines relating to the rights of others and of other proto-communities to share the same freedoms and possibilities. It is here where the cultural, political and social arguments and movements might unite in new ways.[14] The aim would be to recognize all as cultural producers, to understand the different conditions under which symbolic work and creativity occur and to try to strengthen and encourage these conditions, not only to increase choice in consumption, but the choices over choices and to increase the possibilities of creative consumption leading to stronger forms of production. One starting point might be an actually quite modest aim: that every local urban area should have some kind of cultural space or building with relevant technologies and means of production and reproduction devoted in open ways and under whatever institutional rubric to a notion of *cultural possibility*.

This becomes too specific. The crucial general point is the absolute importance of trying to think in future oriented ways guided by tendencies already evident within current common culture. In important measure, the emphasis needs to be shifted from a traditional concern to make *workers* more equal, not simply to make *consumers* more equal, but to equalize the possibilities for us all to become fully developed *cultural producers*. The tasks associated with this are not easy. They loop back, of course, to many 'old' and continuing problems (economic inequalities and exploitation) as well as forwards to many new ones (the likely resistances and exclusions of informal life). But our ideas, actions and politics need to be 'this side', the future side, of common culture, of the reality of the emergence of everyday symbolic work and creativity on widely available and usable cultural materials in the practical experience of the common people. Too many 'progressives', even or perhaps especially when they talk of 'modernism' or 'post-modernism', really speak from the 'other side', the backwards side, of common culture. They see value in 'things' and authority in knowledge of them. They may be past thinking of the common people in terms of a passive mass, but they have not yet understood the importance of the mass of their ordinary creativity for the cultural possibilities of whole societies.

It is contradictory and faulted, on foreign territory viewed from old comforts and certainties, but common culture is our best guide yet to what a cultural commonwealth might look like, or at least will have to contain, not fall back from. Let's look to the streets, to the common culture, not to the towers, for what is to be learnt.

It is in this light that we offer this book and its method to the symbolic work and creativity of our readers.

Notes

1 The term 'common culture' has been used throughout, of course, as a generic term to indicate many actual cultures and cultural forms.
2 An insight first made systematic in the 'cultural industries strategy' of the Greater London Council in the early 1980s.
3 There isn't sufficient space here, but it is interesting to run through and transform in meaning some of the orthodox Marxist categories in relation specifically to cultural commodities. It can certainly be agreed that their use values predominate over their exchange values – or at least have to be understood, as the main text states, in different and more extended ways. Although surplus value can certainly be extracted from the production of cultural commodities, it is far from clear how well the labour theory of value holds up for understanding the exploitation of the primary labour of their production where embodied labour time, however intensified, may be very small.

  More interesting, however, are possible developments to be made in the classic account of the stages of the realization of surplus value in the stages of transformation in the circuit of Capital. In particular it may be possible to work through the circuit from the starting point of (cultural) commodities rather than from Money.

  In Volume 2 of *Capital*, Marx deals extensively with the contradictory dialectic of the circuit between money (capital) and commodities from the point of view of the uneven and crisis-ridden reproduction and expansion of capital (M-C-M'). This formula can, however, be read as depicting the contradictory necessity for capitalism (money) to produce the conditions for the wide availability of cultural commodities as symbolic resources in common culture. If we cycle the formula forward a stage we come to C-M-C'.* That is, the circuit of transformations in the expansion of money can also be understood as a circuit of transformations in *the expansion of cultural commodities*. We may say that just as money has to be converted into commodities in order to enlarge itself, so cultural commodities through their transformation into money are *necessarily* also enlarged. The very necessity of the realization of value through exchange underwrites and enforces the necessity of the consumption of cultural commodities – unlike high art, cultural commodities *have* to be *used* and used ever more widely. The accumulation of capital is also – however contradictorily – the accumulation of culture!

  Also Marx is quite clear that the stages of transformation in the circuit of capital are real and contain risks. Money is not the same

* Suggested by Phil Corrigan in discussion.

stuff as commodities, and there is no guarantee that commodities will be exchanged in order to complete the circuit, but only through taking this risk will capital be enlarged. We may say, therefore, that cultural commodities similarly cannot be understood simply as another form of money – the transformation is real, and money cannot determine the logic of cultural commodities, only seek to ensure their commodity form, exchangeability and *use*. Transformations in the circuit of capital are just that, *transformations*, but the full implications of this for contradictory and uncertain cultural development have not been explored.

4 See, for instance, the writings of the high priest of post-modernism, Jean Baudrillard in his *Selected Writings*, Polity Press, 1988.

5 Reported in *The Times*, 8 February 1989.

6 See Dave Marsh's biography of Bruce Springsteen, *Glory Days*, Arrow, 1988. The points in this and the following note were made by Huw Beynon in conversation.

7 Though Bruce Springsteen may feel frustration and failure in trying to control what he's created, he also remembers very well the educative power and importance of music in his own development. He reports that he learned more from the playing of one three-minute record than from the whole of his schooling. See Dave Marsh, *Glory Days*, op. cit.

8 As Angela McRobbie writes in *New Statesman and Society*, 9 September 1988:

> The new magazines marketed for 16-year-olds and over, but read by thousands of 12-year-olds up and down the county, carry glossy adverts not just for make-up but also for the NatWest, for the Midland Bank, for Levis, pizzas, films, other magazines, for Barclays, Benetton and beyond.

9 See P. Willis *et al.*, *The Youth Review*, Avebury, 1988, for a fuller discussion of 'alternative transitions'.

10 For a recent outline and overview see Dick Hebdige, 'After the masses', *Marxism Today*, January 1989.

11 See, for instance, John Pick, 'Arts under the hammer', *Times Educational Supplement*, 20 January 1989.

12 These contrasts were suggested by Celia Lury in discussion.

13 The Henley Centre for Forecasting (1986) predicts that this collapse will be brought on by the decline in numbers of young adults (24 per cent decline in 15-to-24-year-olds by 1996), continuously high levels of youth unemployment and rising levels of real disposable income among other segments of the population.

14 For a discussion of some of the possibilities in the area of youth work and policy, see P. Willis, op. cit.

Afterword

An early pre-publication response to this text by Simon Frith raised an objection: every aspect of social practice seemed to have been Absorbed by us into 'culture' and infused with an historical romantic glow of creativity leaving no room for questions of textual quality and of the privileged creativity necessary for the production of cultural texts and artefacts.

These are important points and I'll try briefly to indicate a line of response utilizing some terms and approaches first outlined some while ago in my book, *Profane Culture*.[1] I would argue that the present book has not actively exiled the question of comparative quality in texts and artefacts. It has certainly argued that they do not produce automatic effects. They have to be understood in their social relations of consumption. But the social relations of consumption do not supply all meaning. The emphasis on grounded aesthetics and symbolic creativity in everyday life is necessary in order to redress the balance of the whole debate. But there does remain, at least for theoretical adequacy, the need to ask, so to speak, 'from the side of' the artefact or cultural product, which of its internal features relate, and how, to the social possibility and encouragement of grounded aesthetics? What, against the grain of the book, is creative *in* the text? The 'official canon' will not do as a guide to 'quality'. What are the alternative criteria?

The crucial starting point is whether or not and how symbolic artefacts successfully *mediate* social and symbolic meanings and provide the possibilities for the generation of grounded aesthetics. Symbolic artefacts cannot themselves 'contain' the aesthetic fully formed. They can only hope to supply some of the raw materials for this possibility in the necessary symbolic work of the reader or viewer. What determines how far they are able to mediate this possibility? First of all, texts must contain not pure putative 'aesthetics' but raw symbolic material for the reader's or viewer's own symbolic work. The symbolic elements of the text or artefact must be *open* in allowing readers or viewers ample elbow room to make their own selections and appropriations of symbols and meaning. At the same time, however, symbolic resources should represent *homologically* some of the elements of the necessary symbolic work of the receivers already in train: they must be 'passable', relevant. There must be some kind of *homology* between the symbolic resources and meanings of the text and the values, focal concerns, meanings and preoccupations of the receivers. But mediation of meaning does not, itself, guarantee a creative generation of grounded aesthetics. For this we need to entertain the notion of at least a momentary *integration* between text and sensibility, between text and processes of symbolic work within the receiver, including and involving changes in the meanings, understandings, settings and orderings of other, especially experiential, symbolic resources which feed into that work. This is what produces the possibility of new symbolic articulations, of new creative meanings, of further grounded aesthetics.

This is not to posit an idealist or mystical one-ness, but to propose a dialectical notion of *integral circuiting* between processes and structures of the self and elements of text which changes both, lifting and empowering the reader/viewer/listener, and recomposing meanings within the text. This may be a purely mental and emotional operation where a momentary realignment of previous experience and perception allows new appreciations of the text to produce further dialectic re-orderings of meaning 'within the text' – working through, and perhaps simultaneously, subjective feelings of destruction and conflict as well as through affirmation. But this dialectic may also involve a real material re-ordering of symbolic elements or artefacts, as in the generation, *bottom up*, of fashion or sub-culture, so changing or resetting *homologies* to enable further necessary symbolic work, and with it the possibility of further grounded aesthetics.

What, from the side of the text or artefact, might encourage *integral circuiting*? We must maintain an openness here. It's possible that aesthetic effects might flow from 'bad' artefacts. People can use 'bad things' in surprising ways. Sometimes we need 'bad things' to break down and out of old traps and habits. Nevertheless it's reasonable to suggest that the arrangement of symbols in some texts or artefacts might have a greater likelihood of producing and *sustaining* creative responses – from specific groups at least – than in others. Such texts or artefacts are, in some way, symbolically 'pump primed'. There is an *aesthetic tension* between some of its constitutive symbols. This tension concerns both the relationship between, and the particular nature of individual symbols. The unusual or creative choice and combination, or combination or recombination of combinations, of symbols, reflecting in some way perhaps the work of a prior grounded aesthetics, may produce an instability in conventional meaning which facilitates the possibility, therefore, of *creative* recompositions of meanings by *active* consumers (readers, listeners, viewers) in further grounded aesthetics.

Perhaps it helps here to distinguish signs from symbols. Signs are the simple material indicators – sounds, squiggles and dots – of symbolic meaning. If you like, they exist in a cultural limbo. They are not, *themselves*, meaningful. Symbols are signs *plus* their human-given meanings. *Aesthetic tension* between symbols can somewhat detach signs from their given or conventional meanings. This allows the possibility of alternative combinations – for the viewers/readers to do their own 'composing' to provide wider, more suggestive or universal significance. Such unstable symbols related to each other through *aesthetic tension* may be relatively more open than other symbols to the dialectical work of *integration* in real social relationships. Once they've formed into stable *homologies*, however, once they have deposited meanings in certain specific ways, the symbols may settle down into regular and secure meanings for particular audiences.

The possibility of the yeasty (fermentation occurring only in the social process of activation) combination of symbols in a text gives potential power, however little, over reality to creative symbols, even when their original combination comes from grounded aesthetics. They can help to reset the *necessary symbolic work* of viewers and listeners, to make this work more productive of identity, and more likely to encourage grounded aesthetics, more likely to renew creative circuits of meaning between changed sensibilities and practices and the changed meanings of symbols.

In these senses it is possible to talk of the comparative qualities of texts and of the special role of that creativity which makes them.

Another set of objections coming, so to speak, from the other (social) side of grounded aesthetics has arisen in discussion, and can certainly be foreseen. This concerns the overall effect of social, political and ideological relations on the meaning, use and significance of texts and artefacts. From the now orthodox Gramscian perspective, for instance, this book will be criticized for not placing the cultural forms under scrutiny within the continuous struggles of the 'power-block' to maintain its hegemony over the 'popular classes'. This perspective sees the whole of 'popular culture' as a site of struggle within which the particular meanings of texts, signs and symbols change according to larger relations – this year's radical symbol becomes next year's fashion, becomes the following year's nostalgia.

I don't dispute the importance of the notion of hegemony, nor the complexity of the phenomena and questions it tries to encompass. In one way or another these have been my own (micro) questions too – how (objective) subordination is sometimes lived (subjectively) as celebration; why oppressed groups go so lively to their own confinement.[2] But I have never used the term 'hegemony' simply because it seems too general and malleable a concept to be of much use in the analysis of concrete living social practices. I accept, of course, at the highest level of abstraction, the historical specificity of this country in 1989 characterized by capitalist relations of exploitation under regulatory and ideological conditions provided by the social democratic state. But, for me, understanding how these structures remain stable in particular, specified social regions leads to trying to understand, at least in part, how these things are *sensuously* experienced, lived and contradictorily reproduced in ordinary lives – not how abstract hegemony is produced through the medium of ordinary people. The 'power-block' can hardly agree within itself – as the divisions between patrician tories, entrepreneurial Thatcherites and social democratic Kinnockites daily demonstrate – never mind imprint its meanings through a commercial cultural sector which itself is seething with anarchy. The commercial sector finds it more than ever difficult to predict tastes and fashion, never mind to encode dominant meanings in them, except of course and very importantly through the commodity form itself (but see Note 3 of the last chapter). The advertising commentary section of the *Financial Times* is full of weekly laments about the impossibility of predicting or guiding fashion and future taste. This uncertainty is the impetus towards post-Fordist batch production and shorter product development cycle times – not some producer logic for its own sake.

In recent Gramscian analyses of Thatcherism it is far from clear what is supposed to be cause and what effect. Has the Thatcherite hegemony produced post-Fordism and the breakdown of monolithic classes or is it an interpretive and organizing response to them? I would want to insert a much more prosaic, organic, slow moving everyday influence into the debate – common culture has produced increasing numbers of independent and recalcitrant ordinary citizens and voters who are very much more difficult for everybody to handle or understand. Though the evidence is so far very thin concerning actual changes in production, the talk at least of designer products, shorter lead times etc. (post-Fordism) may be a marketing and displaced political *response* to these deep cultural changes, not their cause. They demonstrate failed or slipping hegemony – not new forms of it.

Although Gramscian perspectives developed in part as a critical reaction to structuralism, the emphasis on the external structure of internal signs is, for me at least, very reminiscent of structuralist notions of overdetermination. The problem is that the description of a universal process (despite the claims for historical specificity) gives no clues to the form of the actual sensuous, concrete practices of the cultural level. What makes identity 'from below' and 'horizontally' is crucially missing from most accounts of hegemony. Social agents may not be seen as passive bearers but they still have not become much more than brightly coloured cardboard cut-outs pushed around the hegemony boardgame. No doubt the larger context matters. Fashions and meanings change of course. But so do people, and their own sensuous practices with their own productions at their own level – including fun, joy, meaning-making – are responsible for making many of these changes. Hegemonic perspectives seem to be deeply uninterested in these actual practices and recoup 'popular cultural' contents too quickly into the politics of people/power block relations. There are many oppositions and binary poles dynamically at play in social life which we have not yet developed theoretical forms to uncover. Ethnography of various kinds is important precisely because it records, however incoherently, some of this complexity (or as it is usually described, 'richness') without immediately decanting social experience into larger structural categories. The formulations around grounded aesthetics in this book do not contradict the claims of hegemonic perspectives but attempt the insertion of some awkward dynamic and 'mid-range' concepts which have the capacity to adequately respond to and explain the 'richness' of ethnographic data and which, in my view, no larger perspective can afford to overlook or leave aside.

Of course the difficulty remains with my position – how are the 'liberations' of grounded aesthetics associated with final confinement, how would I work through their social links to the macro *in the other direction* to the usual downward hegemonic routes? In part the very informality of grounded aesthetics is an explanation here. They do not confront or are simply uninterested in power. They have no counter-hegemonic drive or interest. They make their own divisions and oppositions. They are not directly *political*.[3] They accommodate power or find myriad compensations for suffering it – and so help to reproduce it by default. Common culture de-stresses economic power relations by finding and exploring new fields for human capacity and satisfaction. Large parts of common culture are simply indifferent to that system which supplies the products it is certainly not indifferent to.

But I would like to explore finally another line of reasoning – different from the restraints of hegemony – as to why the ordinary people of common culture have not been queuing up to join the left intellectuals in bringing about a social transformation.

A central theme of this book has been how symbolic resources are mobilized through grounded aesthetics for the construction of meaning and identity – a pursuit of a kind of wholeness (individual certainly, more uncertainly, collectively through proto-communities). The wholeness of belonging to larger traditional structures of value, feeling and identity becomes less possible and yet the contradictions and terrible fissures of daily life continue in need of desperate repair – in work, in unemployment, in the family, dealing with authority, power, scarcity and shortage. Ordinary people have not needed an avant-gardism to remind them of rupture. What they have needed but never received is better and freer materials for building security and coherence in their lives. The materials which are now available come from the market. There is a contradictory convergence between aspects of market provision and the tasks of necessary symbolic work and identity formation. People find on the market incentives and possibilities not simply for their own confinement but also for their own development and growth. Though turned inside out, alienated and working through exploitation at every turn, these incentives and possibilities promise more than any visible alternative. Common people may recognize more fully these possibilities – their spices, spaces and freedoms – than does the system itself.

The possibilities and opportunities provided by the market economy can also be *comparatively* evaluated in the 'made messages' of common culture. Not only do the visible socialist alternative models conspicuously fail to offer these things – to ordinary people at least – but they also seem to enforce completely circumscribed, discredited and bankrupt identities. The now-tumbling walls, towers and ideas of the East suggest that their refusal here in the popular mind has other causes and logics than hegemonic domination – indeed they suggest that an important hegemonic question might concern the silences and complicities of some parts of our own left formations.

Of course, the 'counter-hegemonic' struggle has never been about the imposition of an authoritarian state socialism – even though ordinary people are perfectly entitled to make up their own minds about the degenerative potentials of socialism. More important is that the critical or counter-hegemonic impulse can seem profoundly élitist and deconstructive of the possibilities *now* of wholeness. It can seem dismissive of those very cultural materials which hold the prospect of immediate advance and a kind of emancipation. Common culture tells us that identities have to be made before they can be broken. Deconstruction, breaking and interruption are profoundly out of time when the common people have hardly come through to any kind of cultural modernization. Under existing conditions, many counter-hegemonic tendencies can stand justly charged of élitism and social irrelevance.

Nor will it suffice any longer in the face of creative grounded aesthetics to say that modern 'consumer identities' simply repeat 'inscribed positions' within market-provided texts and artefacts. Of course the market does not provide cultural empowerment in anything like a full sense. There are choices, but not choices over choices – the power to set the cultural agenda. Nevertheless the market offers a contradictory empowerment which has not been offered elsewhere. It may not be the best way to cultural emancipation for the majority, but it may open up the way to a better way. Only through some creative control and the exercise – through whatever materials in whatever way – of symbolic faculties and capacities will new demands and new levels of control and mastery be made possible at all.

The point is that the ironies and contradictions here must be recognized and worked through, not thrown up into barricades of hegemony, Berlin walls of contempt and incomprehension around common culture. The simple truth is that it must now be recognized that the coming together of coherence and identity in common culture occurs in surprising, blasphemous and alienated ways seen from old-fashioned Marxist rectitudes – in leisure not work, through commodities not political parties, privately not collectively.

Of course the newly coming-together whole identities of common culture may be recruited to reactionary views (such as, 'We need to do something to curb the Unions') which seem to reproduce some of the conditions for their own domination. But the important point here is the impulse to wholeness and the greater possibilities of recruitment to positions willingly through social independence. Better this by far than an automatic solidarity coming from only partially-developed identities structured in security only by unthinking allegiance. Common culture opens up at least the chance that when rational, human choices do exist they might be rationally made. For the moment, who doesn't make partial choices with uncertain information for different tactical reasons? More than ever now the road to socialism is clouded and uncertain. Who, for instance, doesn't accept with hindsight the inevitability of some of the Thatcherite 'reforms' of the last decade? Is political difference now to be explained, and opposition to be discredited, by the simple application of a stamp reading 'hegemonically determined'?

None of this is to discount an interest in the possibilities of achieving a final human and democratic socialism as something different from common culture. But this will have to be dialectical, unprefigured and working from the (alienated) strengths of common culture. Over-ridingly, ordinary people must make themselves as culturally producing citizens before they make socialism. Meanwhile it should be no surprise that theories and plans for their premature, abstract unmaking are resisted.

Paul Willis

Notes

1 P. Willis, *Profane Culture*, Routledge & Kegan Paul, 1978.
2 P. Willis, *Learning to Labour*, Gower, 1977.
3 These issues are discussed in a political and policy context in P. Willis *et al.*, *The Youth Review*, Avebury, 1988.

Appendix: contributions to the Gulbenkian project from which the present text draws

Juliette Ash: 'Fashion and the clothing industry'.

Ian Connell: 'Youth Statistics'.

Labour Market Studies Group, University of Leicester (Dave Ashton and Malcolm Maguire): 'The cultural responses of young people to unemployment'.

Simon Frith: 'Young people and music'.

Simon Jones: 'Music activity in South Birmingham; style and fashion in young people's lives'.

Celia Lury: 'A study of youth art policies'.

Angela McRobbie: 'Young women, secondhand clothes and style'.

Kobena Mercer: 'Black hair/style politics'.

Graham Murdock: 'Young people and communications technologies: implications for creativity'.

Mica and Orson Nava: 'TV commercials and young people'.

Alan Tomlinson: 'The young consumer – commercial strategies and young people's everyday activity in Britain 1950–1990; voluntary activity, public policy and the cultural activity of young people'.

Derek Walsgrove: 'Creative identity: the role of fantasy in the everyday life of the young unemployed'.

Gary Whannel: 'Young people and sport'.

Janice Winship: 'Young people and magazine culture'.

Index